A Place Apart

A Place Apart

A Pictorial History of Hot Springs, Arkansas

RAY HANLEY

The University of Arkansas Press
Fayetteville
2011

ISBN-10: 1-55728-954-9
ISBN-13: 978-1-55728-954-4

15 14 13 12 11   5 4 3 2 1

Designed by Liz Lester

LIBRARY OF CONGRESS CATALOGING-IN-PUBLICATION DATA

Hanley, Ray, 1951–
        A place apart : a pictorial history of Hot Springs, Arkansas /
    Ray Hanley.
            p.   cm.
        Includes bibliographical references and index.
        ISBN-13: 978-1-55728-954-4 (pbk. : alk. paper)
        ISBN-10: (invalid) 1-55728-945-9
        1. Hot Springs (Ark.)—History. 2. Hot Springs (Ark.)—History—Pictorial
    works. I. Title.
        F419.H8H363   2011
        976.7'41—dc22

                                                            2011010449

To the Garland County Historical Society
and all the people who have worked to preserve
both the historical record of Hot Springs and the
landmark buildings that make up one of the
most distinctive resorts in the nation.

CONTENTS

	Introduction	ix
ONE	Discovery and Exploration	I
TWO	Slow Emergence: 1805–1865	5
THREE	Rising from Ruin: 1865–1880	13
FOUR	Growth and Promise: 1880–1890	25
FIVE	Victorian Splendor: 1890–1900	35
SIX	Opulence, Glamour, and Disaster: 1900–1910	47
SEVEN	Prohibition, War, and a Great Inferno: 1910–1920	61
EIGHT	The Spa City's Roaring Twenties: 1920–1930	81
NINE	Depression, an Expanding Federal Presence, and Slow Recovery: 1930–1940	101
TEN	Political and World Conflicts Impact the Spa City: 1940–1950	113
ELEVEN	Changing Times: 1950–1960	131
TWELVE	The Last Roll of the Dice: 1960–1970	135
THIRTEEN	The Spa City in Its Postgambling Era: 1970–1990	147
FOURTEEN	Bringing a World-Renowned Resort to a Crossroads: 1991 to the Present	155
	Notes	161
	Index	167

INTRODUCTION

I was born in Hot Springs, Arkansas, in 1951, not long after the peak
year of 1946 when just over one million thermal baths had been given.
A century earlier the 1851 census recorded only eighty-four residents
in what was to become one of the best-known Victorian spa resorts
in the world. The path the city took to reach that million-bath pin-
nacle, as well as the course it took after the public stopped subscribing
to the miracles long touted in the thermal waters, makes for some of
the most fascinating history in the state of Arkansas. Hopefully,
through words and photographs the reader will appreciate one of the
most fascinating locales in Arkansas.

The modern city of Hot Springs would be, surely by a different
name, just one of a number of mountain-view communities in Arkansas
if not for the 700,000 gallons of thermal waters that bubble daily from
the sides of the Ouachita Mountains that ring the city. Exactly how the
water is heated and forced up through the cracks and fissures of the
mile-deep layer beneath the city is not certain, but there seems general
agreement that it is very old rainfall, perhaps four hundred years old,
finally making its way back to the surface, heated by some three to five
degrees for every three hundred feet it rises.

Certainly Native Americans were the first humans to see and use
the thermal waters, as evidence suggests the first were present eight to
twelve thousand years ago. Legends abound, including one that says
normally warring tribes put aside their weapons when sharing the thermal waters to heal aches and battle wounds. By the time the Europeans
came on the scene, the Quapaw and Caddo tribes were present in the
area. Undocumented stories passed down for four hundred years say
Spanish explorer Hernando de Soto led the first Europeans into the valley of the hot springs. Regardless who arrived first, it would be France
and Spain who would swap back and forth the vast area that included
the hot springs until the United States acquired it as part of the
Louisiana Purchase in 1804.

The potential to turn the valley of the springs into a spa resort was
an off-and-on effort for much of the first half of the nineteenth

century. Travel was difficult, but each year more people made the effort that by 1859 involved a steamboat to reach Little Rock and then a stagecoach on rough-hewn roads to Hot Springs. Real momentum toward the goal of becoming a famous spa resort was halted by the Civil War, which saw the town burned and abandoned.

Hot Springs rose from the ashes of the Civil War and by the 1890s was one of the grandest Victorian resorts in the nation, if not the world. Filled with grand hotels, some with hundreds of rooms, and elegant bathhouses, the city drew thousands with the coming of rail service. The bathing craze might be best captured in the words of Stephan Crane, author of *The Red Badge of Courage,* who visited in 1895. Crane wrote of the bathhouses, "Abodes of peculiarly subdued and home-loving millionaires. . . . Crowds swarm in these baths. A man becomes a creature of three conditions. He is about to take a bath—he is taking a bath—he has taken a bath."

The marketing of the thermal waters, aided greatly by the railroads and even the U.S. government on whose property the springs actually sat, carried the message that little of what ailed a person could not be cured by bathing and drinking the water from the springs. A Missouri Pacific Railroad pamphlet proclaimed in 1910, "It is well to have a Mecca somewhere on earth for the cure of those who suffer cutaneously and viscerally. . . . We have found such a place, such a body of water rushing from the generous centers of nature."

The U.S. secretary of war wrote in a brochure in 1909, "Generally speaking, all diseases of the skin, blood, digestive, and secretory organs, and nervous affections and ailments peculiar to women, . . . may be cured or benefited. . . . Troubles that yield most readily to the hot water treatment are: alcoholism, catarrh, chronic insomnia, kidney and liver troubles, chronic diarrhea, malaria, nervous prostration, locomotor ataxia, paralysis, psoriasis, rheumatism, stomach diseases, tobacco poisoning, etc."

The heyday of the resort was captured by photographers from the boom of the 1870s onward, and it is this rich pictorial history that offers a wonderful look into what the city was. By contrast today, the images show that much has been lost from the fires, floods, and rush of American business enterprise to tear down the unique, the historical, and the serviceable to build functional but bland new buildings or, in too many cases in Hot Springs, a parking lot. One of the major goals of this book is to walk the reader through the pictorial history of the city.

As the twentieth century moved toward the decades of WWI and the Roaring Twenties, Hot Springs entrepreneurs expanded their offerings to include horse racing, alligator and ostrich farms, baseball, and, on the darker side, wide-open gambling and other vices including prostitution. The twenties and thirties would see the city become a favorite for gangsters from northern cities drawn by the tolerant ways of the spa city.

Each decade has seen changes, sometimes brought on by world-shaking events. World War II expanded the military presence in the city where the Army and Navy Hospital loomed over the downtown tourist district. Other changes came with the advent of modern medicine, which caused ever fewer people to believe in the thermal waters' ability to cure their ailments and restore their health. Some changes were directed out of the state capitol in Little Rock, as a series of governors made half-hearted efforts to end the gambling that remained a tourist draw after the steady decline of the bathing business after WWII. The roulette wheels, rolling dice, and clanging slot machines would only be silenced for good by Governor Winthrop Rockefeller in 1967.

Over the past forty years, since gambling ended, Hot Springs has gone through stagnation to emerge as a year-round family-centered destination seeking to balance new attractions with a sometimes uphill struggle to preserve its historic architectural legacy. It is hoped that this book will be part of a renewal of interest in preserving perhaps the most distinctive destination in Arkansas.

The artist depicts an unsubstantiated story that de Soto, being shown a thermal spring here, actually visited the hot springs in 1542. *Courtesy of Garland County Historical Society*

CHAPTER ONE

Discovery and Exploration

The history of the valley of the hot springs prior to the late 1600s is speculation, but we know the first visitors were native American tribes, though no written records exist to tell us which tribes were present or when they first arrived. There is legend about visits from Spanish explorers like de Soto but no records to document if they actually set foot in the area.

Recorded history does document that France was the next, if not the first, European group to attempt to conquer the Mississippi River valley and the area encompassing today's Arkansas. In 1682 French explorer René-Robert Cavelier de La Salle, better known in history books as just La Salle, claimed for King Louis XIV all the lands drained by the Mississippi River, and thus the area around the hot springs. The vast territory was ceded back and forth between Spain and France more than once, but it would be Napoleon that held it in 1802 when Thomas Jefferson set his sights on New Orleans.

Jefferson and his advisors wanted to give the young American nation control of at least the lower Mississippi River on its western border. With that goal Jefferson dispatched his delegate Robert Livingston to France to attempt to purchase Louisiana along with New Orleans. Livingston carried in his possession the president's authorization to spend up to $10 million to acquire control of the lower Mississippi River.

While Mr. Livingston was disembarking in France, Napoleon was preoccupied with issues closer to home. France was on the verge of going to war with Great Britain, who ruled the seas with its mighty navy. Napoleon reasoned that his inferior navy could not maintain control of its North American empire, especially if the United States allied itself with Great Britain. Napoleon was in a mood to sell a lot of real estate.

Rather than just buying Louisiana, Napoleon suggested the United States pay $15 million for the entirety of the French possessions; this became known as the Louisiana Purchase and immediately doubled the size of the United States. Thus, in accepting the French leader's offer, the United States came to have within its borders what would one day become Hot Springs National Park.

President Jefferson was eager to have explored the vast new lands he had acquired for the nation. The well- chronicled two-year journey of Lewis and Clark, who traversed the Great Plains and the Rockies and ended on the shores of the Pacific Ocean, provided ample evidence of this president's drive to explore. However, Jefferson had also read accounts of those who had visited the fabled "hot springs of the Washita" hidden deep in the mountains of Arkansas, and he determined to learn more about this part of his vast acquisition.

Jefferson enlisted the services of William Dunbar, a Natchez-area plantation farmer, amateur scientist, and native of England, who would lead an expedition to evaluate the area of the hot springs.

Armed with a budget of three thousand dollars appropriated by the Congress, and having secured the services of chemist George Hunter, Dunbar set out with thirteen soldiers, two of his own slaves, and his teenage son. The small band traveled up the Red River and then up the Washita River (later to be called Ouachita) seeking the hot springs of which Dunbar had heard tales of miraculous healing properties.

Dunbar's group arrived in the vicinity of present-day Malvern, Arkansas, some twenty-five miles from Hot Springs, on December 5, 1804. The soldiers bagged turkeys and even shot at the buffalo that roamed the area's open meadows. They did not linger long but soon proceeded up the Washita until they rode into the valley of rising vapors emanating from dozens of hot springs found on the slopes of mountains dormant in winter. The area was deserted upon Dunbar's arrival, but the hand of civilization had already left its mark. The group's journals described "an open log cabin and a few huts of split boards, all calculated for summer encampments, which had been erected by persons resorting to the springs for the recovery of their health."[1]

Dunbar's expedition, being the first well-organized and fully equipped group to visit the springs, spent the rest of December 1804 studying the area. Hunter, the scientist, measured the water temperature of what he considered the major springs, recording readings ranging from 132 to 150 degrees Fahrenheit. Walking up the creek fed by hot water coming from fractured rocks upstream, Dunbar noted, "At intervals the water oozes out or drips from the bank into the creek, which during the present cool season is very evident from the condensed vapor which floats along the margin of the creek."[2]

Dunbar arrived safely back home in Natchez and submitted his report to President Jefferson, along with carefully prepared maps of the area. The president would include details of the expedition in his address to Congress in February 1806. Little was noted in the press of the president's brief mention of the hot springs in his remarks. However, contained in the journal notes of Dunbar's party were the first recorded details of a bath in the mystical waters. One of the men, having been ill, noted how he lay in a heated pool in the creek at its juncture with a hot spring with a blanket over himself, drinking the hot mineral water until breaking out into a deep sweat. He then took a plunge in the cold December creek above the heated inflow. The man repeated this ritual several times a day for two weeks. He reported feeling much stronger for the process and was able to resume hunting with his companions.

The healing properties of the hot springs nestled in the vast unexplored wilderness of Arkansas had been recorded on paper for the first time with this first documented series of Hot Springs bath treatments. Little did the unidentified man in Dunbar's party know what would follow that first bathing testimonial over the next century.

CHAPTER TWO

Slow Emergence
1805–1865

Hot Springs' evolution from a wilderness Indian hunting ground to a world-renowned spa would slowly get underway within a few short years after William Dunbar's report to President Jefferson. General Zebulon Pike of the U.S. Army, while exploring the Arkansas River, dispatched a part of his command south and for the first time literally placed the hot springs on the map.

The first permanent settlement around the springs came in either 1807 or 1811, as accounts differ on the arrival of Emanuel Prudhomme, a planter from Natchitoches, Louisiana, who came to seek a cure for his perceived failing health and erected a rough cabin near the springs. Prudhomme pronounced himself cured after two years of thermal baths and transferred his cabin to two trappers from Alabama, John Perciful and Isaac Cates. The men erected the valley's first crude bathtubs near the springs, and by 1810 they were hosting visitors in small numbers during the summer months.

By 1819, the year before the Arkansas Territory was carved away from the Missouri Territory, there were fairly well-blazed trails through the thick timber into the area of the hot springs, mostly from the south out of Louisiana. Thomas Nutall, a botanist from England, traveled the route up from Natchitoches to what is now Monroe, Louisiana, and up the Ouachita River from there.

During his stay Nutall wrote of the first efforts to harvest the healing waters.

> It is only after mixing with the cool water of the brook, at some distance from this spring, that it becomes of a temperature in which it is possible to bathe. There is, however, a kind of rude enclosure made around the spring, as a steam bath, which often probably debilitates and injures the health of ignorant and emaciated patients.[1]

The first record of a hotel in the valley of the springs was a "dogtrot log cabin" built in 1820 by Joseph Mellard; this was the first structure intended to provide lodging for a fee. By the time thirty-six-year-old Mr. Ludovicus Belding, a veteran of the War of 1812, arrived in 1828 Mellard's crude log hotel was gone, and the valley was empty. Belding had come to stay, though, and he would leave his mark on the area. The Massachusetts native, along with his wife Lydia and three children, had traveled from Indiana by wagon over rough, almost impassable roads.

Belding saw a great future for the hot springs, so he built and opened a hotel. Then he made more history in 1832 when his wife gave birth to the first white child born in the area.

In August 1829 the *Gazette* recorded the testimonial of one visitor to the springs, who praised the waters' healing properties but not the surroundings. "They have produced extraordinary cures in rheumatism, paralysis, liver complaint, enlargement of the spleen, eruptions, pulmonary complaints, obstructions, and chronic disorders of every kind." The man also offered the first testimony of the waters' power to heal venereal disease, most likely syphilis. "Where the system has been saturated with mercury which has been imperfectly purged out, they will salivate again after a great lapse of time to carry off the mercury. Old and fixed venereal taints are also eradicated by their use."[2] In the era before any antibiotics, one accepted treatment for syphilis was to rub mercury into the skin of the infected person. Bathing in thermal waters was thought to purge the body of the mercury, and hopefully the syphilis.

In April 1832 Ambrose H. Sevier, serving as delegate for the Arkansas Territory in Congress, filed legislation laying claim to the springs for the federal government. "And be it further enacted, that the hot springs in said territory, together with four sections of land including said springs shall be reserved for the future disposal of the United States, and shall not be entered, located, or appropriated for any other purpose whatever."[3] The legislation passed, but it would take years of debate and a maze of legal proceedings before the ownership would be settled. That same year, the *Arkansas Gazette* reported that the average number of visitors to the hot springs had reached four hundred for the year. Unlike past years, as winter approached some of the arrivals chose to stay in the valley. Indeed,

1832 was perhaps the most eventful year since the arrival of the first Europeans in the valley of the hot springs. It was said to be the "first real season," with a number of well-to-do planters coming from Louisiana. Gen. Sam Houston was reported to have visited for an entire month of bathing.

In June 1832 Hiram Abiff Whittington, a pioneer who would leave a strong mark on the area, arrived at the springs where he obtained a two-room log cabin and opened a store with a total of five hundred dollars to his name. Whittington announced the opening of his store, apparently the first in the hot springs valley, with an ad in the *Arkansas Gazette* on February 4, 1834. In the ad he pledged to "constantly keep on hand an assortment of Dry goods, Groceries, Hardware, Glassware and an assortment of Medicines."[4]

One of the surviving letters that Whittington sent to his brother back in Massachusetts in 1832 sheds a bit more light on the bachelor's initial living arrangements.

> I live here in a little cabin of logs about ten feet square with an adjoining room about seven by nine feet. The larger room is my store room, clerk's office, post office, bed chamber, etc. My bed, table, two trunks and a box with a small stool comprise my household furniture, and on a shelf in the corner is my library. . . . There is a beautiful stream running within five yards of my door, and all I have to do is to get up in the morning, step to this purling brook and wash my eyes open and the drudgery of my day's work is done. My boarding house is on the opposite side of the street. I walk across three times a day and come back, take a book, throw myself on a cot and read away the time. Now and then a mountaineer will trot in, dressed in his leather hunting shirt and leggings. He will inquire what's going on in the world of Arkansas, buy a few goods at a hundred percent on a twelve month credit to be paid in bear oil, bear skins, etc. and take his departure. Did you ever hear of anything like it?[5]

Late November 1834 saw the arrival of English scientist and proclaimed world traveler George W. Featherstonhaugh (pronounced "Fanshaw"), a U.S. government geologist. The War Department had appointed him that year to make a geological survey of the Arkansas Territory.

Featherstonhaugh and his son made a three-day wagon trip from

Little Rock to reach the springs. Featherstonhaugh recorded in his journals his first sight of the valley of the hot springs.

> Four wretched-looking log cabins, in one of which was a small store [that of Hiram Whittington], contained all the accommodations that these springs offered to travelers. We had never seen anything worse or more unpromising than they were, but driving up to the store, a Mr. Whittington, who purchases bear skins and other skins of wild animals of the hunters, paying for them in the commodities he gets from Little Rock, and who did not seem in a very promising way to the Lord Mayoralty of London, was obliging enough to say we might take possession of one of the log cabins. Having taken care of our horse we accordingly moved into the first that we had passed on our arrival. It had a roof to it as well as a little portice, as a defense against the rays of the sun, but this was literally all that it had, for not an article of furniture was there either in the shape of a chair or table. The floor was formed of boards roughly and unevenly hewn, and, unfortunately some of them were wanting. Being reckoned, however, the best lodging in the place, we made the best of it, and through our new friend got skins, blankets, and other appliances to serve as bedding. We next laid in some firewood and constructed a kind of table, so that when we had succeeded in borrowing two old chairs, we looked with some satisfaction upon our new attempt at housekeeping. We were sure at any rate of being alone, and of being out of the reach of filth of every kind; in fact it was *almost* as desirable as being in the woods, and had the advantage of shelter. How invalids contrive to be comfortable, who come to this ragged place, I cannot imagine, yet I understand that ten or a dozen people are often crammed into this room, which my son and myself found much too small for two. Persons who resort to these springs in the autumn might do well if they brought with them their own tents and a sack or two of flour, for meat in the latter part of year is abundant and of good quality, which is not at other times when the animals are breeding and suckling their young.[6]

The first night Featherstonhaugh lodged in a leaky cabin in a downpour while hogs rooted beneath the plank floor. He would leave ten days later in good spirits though with what he needed to later make a report to the War Department.

In 1835 changes were beginning to occur in the architecture of the hot springs settlement, which up to that time had been made up of log cabins with no special features. The valley's first sawmill opened that summer, making available for the first time lumber and some mill-wright details to dress up the new buildings.

The year 1836, in which Arkansas achieved statehood, saw William Barkeloo of Little Rock put into service a four-horse, nine-passenger carriage to begin service to Hot Springs and other places in the state "when roads permit." By 1838 regular stagecoach service was advertised, offering triweekly trips from Little Rock to Hot Springs. The improved transit resulted in a greater number of both able-bodied and invalid visitors making the trip to the springs. The *Arkansas Gazette* on June 27, 1838, reported that a "large number of invalids" at the springs made plans for the Fourth of July, complete with a reading of the Declaration of Independence. The stagecoaches of Wilson and Thorn adopted a dependable schedule, departing Little Rock each Tuesday and Friday in 1841. The fare, each way, was set at six dollars for a trip that could still take up to two days, on roads that turned to a quagmire in rainy weather.[7]

The number of "invalids" visiting the springs to take the thermal bath treatments began to swell, and by 1844 families were starting to offer accommodations in their homes, in a prelude to the boarding houses that would come later. A. J. and A. Sabin advertised in the *Gazette* "a house for the accommodation of invalids."[8]

The first record of a church building in the area was found in an 1848 account written by a man whose name was listed as just "Bally." After a wedding celebration the night before, Bally attended church services on Sunday morning. His observations were captured in New York's *Spirit of the Times,* a "Publication of Southwest Humor."

> The place of worship was well ventilated, being a new and well-built log house, minus the "chinking," windows and doors. It being rather a blustering day, the pastor labored under considerable difficulty in keeping his text before him, the leaves of the book blowing to and fro, as the breeze changed. To obviate this he drew his "Bowie" knife from the back of his neck and deposited it on one side of the text book. But this would not suffice; the opposite side required "holding down" likewise, and he was compelled to search for his "derringer" and lay that down also. Here was a spectacle, truly! But as all was well now, the pastor went on with the sarmint.[9]

The year 1850 saw the first physician to locate to Hot Springs on a permanent basis: William H. Hammond. A Little Rock newspaper,

True Democrat, estimated in May 1854 that three thousand people visited the springs annually.[10] The *Arkansas Gazette* listed the arrivals at Stidham's Hotel for the period March 15 to June 11; this compilation reflected visitors from seventeen states, as far away as New York. Fifteen slaves were reported to have accompanied their masters to Hot Springs during that time.[11]

The trip by then could be made in twelve hours on ever-improving roads. Many visitors came by riverboat to Little Rock and then caught the stage to Hot Springs.

Advertisement continued to increase, and in 1857 Stidham purchased the Rector House hotel to go with his other establishments. Efforts to maximize revenue saw at least four hotels running identical ads that offered accommodations for "diseased Negroes."[12] Presumably the disease was syphilis, for which the bath treatments were thought to successfully treat, in conjunction with mercury treatments.

The Fourth of July, 1859, was celebrated, according to the *Gazette,* in a way that was "creditable to the getters up of the celebration and those who participated in it."[13]

The gaiety of 1859 and the grand toasts to the United States were perhaps tinged with irony. Although the revelers may have been convinced that good times for Hot Springs had come to stay, it was not to be. Far from the mountain-fringed springs, the health-seekers and the gay parties, a dark cloud was moving over the United States—the distant rumble that would culminate in the American Civil War.

Henry Rector, one of the men who had staked a dubious claim on the hot springs, and who at one point had operated a hotel in the resort town, was elected governor of Arkansas in 1860 and helped lead Arkansas out of the Union in the spring 1861. The war's impact on Hot Springs would eventually be most severe. Union troops moved into Arkansas in 1862, winning a major battle at Pea Ridge. With rumors strong that a Yankee invasion of Little Rock was imminent, Governor Rector moved his staff and the state records to Hot Springs on May 6, 1862. The governor occupied rooms at the Rector House hotel, near what is today the Arlington Park lawn. By July, however, the rumors had subsided, and the governor and his staff returned to Little Rock. Hot Springs had been, for a brief two months, the capital of Arkansas.

Neither Union nor Confederate forces ever occupied Hot Springs during the war, but the lines were thought to be coming close in September 1863 when the Confederate government fled Little Rock, just ahead of the invading Union forces of Gen. Frederick Steele. Fearing that their city would be next in the path of the oncoming Yankees, most of the residents of Hot Springs fled the city, most going to Texas and Louisiana. Reportedly only three white persons remained in Hot Springs during the remainder of the war, along with just a few black servants.

Skirmishes came close to Hot Springs during the war, but the greatest threat came from neither army. With most able-bodied men away at war, bands of outlaw gangs ranged far and wide, robbing, burning, and murdering those who got in their way. The mostly vacant homes and stores of Hot Springs were defenseless in their path, and by the war's end little more than ashes and rubble remained in the valley of the hot springs. The gaiety of that festive Fourth of July in 1859 surely seemed like another century as the former residents straggled home after the war ended in April 1865.

Hot Springs would not fade away into the surrounding forests, however, but like the mythical phoenix, it would eventually rise from the ashes. Its journey towards becoming a world-class resort had been interrupted but not ended.

CHAPTER THREE

Rising from Ruin
1865–1880

The Civil War was over, and former residents began to return to Hot Springs where they found their town had been left in ruins by marauding outlaws during the war. New residents followed, along with a growing stream of visitors that included many maimed soldiers of both the Union and Confederate armies coming to soak their wounds. By 1870, five years after the town had been abandoned, 1,276 people called Hot Springs home.[1] Among them were returning pioneers Hiram Whittington, who was renting rooms again; George Belding, who had rebuilt a store; and John C. Hale, a bathhouse proprietor.

A Woman's View

In the winter of 1867, only two years after the Civil War had laid waste to the area, a young woman named Julia Roane made a three-day trip by wagon from Pine Bluff to Hot Springs. Some eighty-two years later in 1949, her yellowed, tattered diary surfaced, bringing to light her experiences in and impressions of the battered resort town.

> Well, on our arrival after waiting a while, amusing ourselves watching the cloudy vapor rising from the warm water under the bridge which separated the baths from the office, we were conducted to the baths, each separating and going to the appointed one. I had never seen anything of the kind before but thought it would never do to show signs of fear, so went bravely to work to enjoy the fun. There were long wooden troughs about two feet high, a cold water spout and a rope to let in the hot water. I pulled the string and hot foaming water came plunging like a cataract down, loud as the report of a cannon. I thought so and with a bound I was out of the tub and on the floor, the rope dangling about as unconcerned as you please. I got back quickly and stood at one corner pulling the

rope gently with much apprehension as to the probability of the whole concern getting out of order and putting an end to my existence, but after everything was fixed to my notion, I enjoyed my bath very much.

I then entered the vapor bath but could not stand it, it affected my lungs, and I thought it best to get out as soon as possible. This room opened into my bath, it was built over the spring. Narrow planks being placed about one and half inches apart to allow vapor to rise, no air. I stood it as long as possible, great drops or streams of perspiration streamed from my whole body and I was becoming terribly exhausted. Aunt, who was in the next bath, called to me not to stay too long, so I bounced into my tub, gave a brave pull on the rope and after the excitement got into my clothes, took a tin cup of hot water from the bucket which had been put in my room, then we all went back to the Sumpter.[2]

In September 1875 almost a hundred correspondents from various newspapers were enticed to make a trip from St. Louis, traveling south to visit a number of towns across Arkansas. Hot Springs was on the list for the delegation and required train and stagecoach transport. The journalists recorded the experience—complete with a pistol shot—of a "robber" attempting to hold up the stage, which had been added just as entertainment, with someone hired to impersonate a desperado.

We were driven to Hot Springs over the worst road in America, but arriving at the springs our bruises were speedily forgotten in the warm bath provided for us, and the hearty welcome from the citizens of the town. . . . We knew that anyone trying to reach it must be dragged twenty-six miles over rough hilly country. We had tried it out and didn't think that very many invalids could survive the task. We had looked for third-class hotels, second-class doctors, and first-class invalids. We found (instead) a city lighted with gas, supplied with a dozen better hotels than many Northern cities twice its size. We found a street railway three miles long and a city large enough to support a daily newspaper. After a bath in the hot springs waters, the party sat down to a fine dinner, and then off to the Arlington Hotel where a grand reception greeted the visiting delegation.[3]

The most important development of the post–Civil War decade was the final settlement of the ownership of the springs. Amid claims

In the 1870s rare photographs captured views of open springs used for bathing and drinking before the development that would come later. In this condition the water often became polluted and the area around the springs trampled. *Courtesy of Garland County Historical Society*

Hot Springs was almost completely destroyed during the Civil War, mostly by marauding bandits. The following decade saw rapid development, with wagon trains arriving bearing both settlers and those intent on recapturing their health. The three-story Sumpter House hotel was the largest at the time. *Courtesy of Garland County Historical Society*

and counterclaims, the question of who was the rightful owner of the hot springs for decades was widely cited as the main factor holding back the development of the area. An act of Congress in 1870 paved the way for settlement in 1876 at the hands of the U.S. Supreme Court, which weighed the merit of several individual claims against the 1832 congressional legislation that had set aside the springs and four sections of land for "later disposal" by the government.

The contest before the Court pitted some of the best known names in Hot Springs history, Henry Rector (represented by Albert Pike), John C. Hale, the heirs of Ludovicus Belding, and those of John Perciful, who had arrived in the valley in 1809. All were to be disappointed when on April 24, 1876 the Court handed down an order that read, "We feel bound to decide that none of the claimants are entitled to the land in question." Hale and Rector were granted land elsewhere in the city, but the hot springs and the adjacent land was to be public property beyond challenge after the ruling. Finally resolving who owned what land was the spark that would lead to the building of hotels and other accommodations to deliver on the promise many felt Hot Springs held for decades.[4]

A Northerner's View of the City

In January 1878 Hot Springs was afforded nationwide exposure with a sixteen-page article in *Harper's Magazine* written by a journalist named Van Cleaf.[6]

Van Cleaf paused in the street and recorded his first view of the city: "It consists of one long, irregular street called Valley Street, which crosses and recrosses the little stream (Hot Springs Creek). At one part the picturesque little valley is so narrow that the street takes up most of the level, the houses on one side being built over the creek and almost into the mountainside, which in many places has been cut into and blasted away to make room for the buildings and other improvements."

The article sought to explain how the waters of the "Arkansas Bethesda" worked. Cures attributed were of "the skin and blood, nervous affections, rheumatism, and the various diseases of women." Van Cleaf described the treatment as "drinking and bathing in the water and in their steam, producing in each case a profuse perspiration, which is an active agent in the elimination of the disease by natural channels." The article added that it was often necessary to seek the advice of a physician in using the waters, which "if rashly used, are as powerful in breaking down the constitution as they are in building it up. In many cases the system has to be prepared for the treatment by a course of medicine. . . . The hot baths are usually taken once a day for three weeks, when a rest is necessary, and then a second three weeks course." This explanation offered readers an understanding of the need for the rapidly expanding bustling hotels and the hawkers at the depot seeking to sign up incoming visitors with local physicians.

Surprising to Van Cleaf was the perceived benefit of drinking the hot water: "Curiously, the hot water can be drunk almost boiling, as

A *Harper's* reporter in 1878 marveled at the magnificent view from atop the wooden observation tower, writing, "From the tower's observatory a magnificent view can be had of the picturesque watering-place." The Woolman Tower shown here would be the first of three to crown Hot Springs Mountain over a period of 130 years.[6]

it comes from the earth, without any feeling of nausea affecting the drinker. It is tasteless and odorless, and certainly drinking hot water would hardly seem a pleasure. Strange as it may seem, however, a sort of fascination about it, and you find yourself, even if not under treatment, drinking two or three cupfuls in succession."

Making observations of the bathers, the writer noted, "The treatment in general at the hot springs has a very rejuvenating effect, and the faded beauty blooms again after a short residence. Though the springs are visited by many *roués*, both young and old, who come to them to get rid of the effects of their wild course of life, they become very quiet members of society while doing penance."

"Diamond Joe" Reynolds, a New York Quaker who had taken the uncomfortable stage ride, put the Malvern stagecoach out of business when he completed his narrow-gauge railroad between Hot Springs and the Malvern junction station in 1875. Reynolds, whose nickname came from his diamond stickpin, invested heavily in the construction of the twenty-six-mile rail line. The club car of the richly appointed train was staffed with uniformed waiters. The fare started out at $2.50 in 1875 and later dropped to $1.10.[8] Passengers arriving at Hot Springs on the narrow-gauge railroad alighted at this station, often surrounded by agents for area hotels, bathhouses, doctors and drug stores, all seeking to steer business to where they got a commission. *Courtesy of Garland County Historical Society*

Harper's journalist Van Cleaf took note of enterprising residents who mined the quartz crystals outside Hot Springs and brought the diamond-like rocks into the city to sell to visitors. "Crystal hunters bring in wagon-loads of magnificent specimens. Some of the blocks, glittering with thousands of various-sized pointed hexagonal prisms, are as large as two or three feet square. Nearly every visitor buys or mines for himself some specimens of Arkansas diamonds."

Despite being critical of the largely wooden construction of the town's buildings, Van Cleaf found Hot Springs "well provided with excellent hotels, and any number of boarding houses of all prices, restaurants, and saloons. The tables are usually very well supplied, game of all kinds being abundant, and splendid fish being brought from the neighboring Ouachita River."

After interviews and observation around town, Van Cleaf took issue with the town's physicians, noting that many reported cures were achieved solely by bathing and drinking the water, without use of a physician, and concluded that "the doctors give too much medicine in conjunction with treatment by the waters. The drug stores do an

The enterprising crystal sellers Van Cleaf witnessed the birth a permanent industry in 1878, as seen in this photograph around 1940. The massive crystal sold for $250; today it would sell for thousands.

extremely thriving trade, and the amount of medicine seen in the rooms of your invalid friends is enough to sicken a well man." Observing doctors on the crowded Bathhouse Row, the visitor penned, "A doctor passes up the street, sniffing his nose in air as he encounters the patients of a rival." His disdain for the professed healing profession only got deeper the longer he studied the city: "Physicians of all kinds abound at the Springs, from able practitioners to the veriest quacks. As a safe rule, never employ one whose agent has approached you, or whose circular has been handed on nearing the Springs. There is an immense field for quackery, and it is worked to its fullest extent." It would be years before the state made serious efforts to license or regulate physicians in Arkansas.

Later in the week Van Cleaf took notice of the town's churches, including Episcopal, Methodist, Catholic, and both white and black Baptist "chapels." The journalist seemed more intrigued by the black churches, noting that "revivals are very popular among the colored 'bredden' and 'sistern' at the dark Baptist church, and on the long summer afternoons their church melodies are borne up the valley on the breeze." He sat one evening and recorded the words to a hymn:

M'soul shall shine like a star in de mornin,'
Oh, m' little soul's gwine to rise an' shine.
I'll meet my modder at de new buryin'-ground,
Waitin' to honah de Lord.
As I pass by de gates of hell.[8]

Progress seemed to pick up its pace after *Harper's* critical article; the city successfully applied for status as a city of the second class, with a mayor and alderman. Investment was flowing in, building plans were everywhere, and the future was bright—at least until the next major setback, which struck in the early morning hours of March 5, 1878, in the form of a fiery plague that would too often strike Hot Springs. The *Hot Springs Illustrated Monthly News* recorded the story: "What was yesterday a beautiful little city with life and enterprise, was now a scene of charred and smoldering ruins."[9] A kerosene lamp in a "negro shanty back of the French Restaurant," an establishment known as Greenleaf's, had overturned, and the resulting fire spread rapidly up and down the narrow valley of Hot Springs' business district. The city's single horse-drawn fire wagon was of no avail. By the time the fires were out eight hours later, 150 buildings were gone, including City Hall and the offices of the *Sentinel* newspaper, the police and fire stations, and many of the hotels. Fortunately, the larger hotels like the Arlington and the Avenue in the northern end of the valley were spared.

The elected city leaders sought to do their part to help the town recover and soon saw it beset with a building boom. Sidewalks were laid, a new city hall built, and a city park laid out. Five policemen were employed to patrol the sometimes rowdy city, and fines were imposed: drunkenness would cost $1, fighting the same, leaving your horse unhitched $2, and gambling $5. To fund city improvements, business levies included $15 on restaurants, $30 on boarding houses, and $25 on pawn brokers. Banks and liquor stores paid the city $100, first-class hotels $300, and shooting galleries $300.[10]

The *Hot Springs Illustrated Monthly* in February 1878 offered a reference, and advice, on the city's questionable reputation. "As a matter of course, as in all other places of similar character, there are some bad characters, and many gambling houses. But no visitor need subject himself to a dangerous contact with these bad characters unless he voluntarily chooses to do so."[11]

Though recovering from both Civil War and a devastating fire, Hot Springs was optimistic at the end of the decade, as the federal government took leadership in improving the areas around the springs. The stage was set for the 1880s, a decade that would bring Hot Springs, Arkansas, to the brink of its glory as a Victorian resort.

New York native Charles Cutter began spreading Hot Springs' fame far and wide when he started publishing an annual guide to the spa city in 1874. In his first edition he appealed to women to visit: "When the beautiful ladies, and those who would become beautiful, fully understand the effects of these baths upon the skin and complexion, their numbers will increase yearly, until thousands who have ruined their complexion by the excessive use of cosmetics will visit Hot Springs to renew the beauty of youth. Those who feel the heavy hand of time being placed upon them, and their looking glass reveals wrinkles and mole patches, can by bathing in and drinking of these waters, so improve their complexion as to appear several years younger than their actual age."[2]

CHAPTER FOUR

Growth and Promise
1880–1890

The census for Hot Springs in 1880 recorded a population of 3,554, but by 1890 it would rise to over 9,000 amid a decade of growth and grandeur unparalleled up to that time.[1] The first telephone came in 1880 when Western Union ran an iron wire from W. J. Little's grocery store on Central Avenue to Little Rock. By 1884 the city counted 150 telephones. Gas streetlights, which had appeared in 1878, were replaced by new electric street lights by 1882. Mule-drawn streetcars were running under the new lights on tracks granted lease by the city. Progress was breaking out all over town.

Hot Springs may have gotten its biggest booster when New Yorker Charles Cutter arrived to restore his failing health. He began to publish an annual booklet, *Guide to Hot Springs*, in 1874, giving reviews of hotels, bathhouses, and entertainment venues. He also sought to allay concerns about crime and vice that sometimes tainted the resort city's image.

In the four years that elapsed between his 1882 and 1886 guides, Cutter heralded the city's progress, telling potential visitors that the city had "7,000 residents, a Mayor, Police Judge, Chief of Police, one of the best in the land, and a police force of six to ten men. Our visiting population is from the best society to be found in the country, including capitalists, judges, senators, cabinet officers, congressmen and very frequently accompanied by their families." Cutter made other thinly veiled references to imply that the once burgeoning trade in gambling and prostitution had been cleaned up. "The moral standing of the place has been very much improved within the past year. The removal of many annoyances and bad characters is permanent, and the best people now rule."[3] Cutter digresses at one point from how invalids are made well to speak to wayward young men. "No one can come

Valley Street (now Central Avenue) is seen here from a balcony of the Arlington Hotel with a horse-drawn streetcar moving up the dirt street. The streetcar service was started in 1874 when Daniel Butterfield incorporated the Hot Springs Street Railway Company. He laid down the tracks and started with two cars that had been shipped to Malvern by rail and then dismantled and transported over the rough road to Hot Springs on ox carts. *Courtesy of Arkansas History Commission*

to the Hot Springs without receiving a good moral lesson. Parents would do well to send their wild boys to this school. If they would not learn wisdom here there is but little hope of preventing their sowing wild oats. The very restraint I now feel in writing plainly all I would wish to say on this subject is the cause of much of the misery of the world. *Parents, be candid and speak freely to your children; do not allow them to suffer through ignorance.*"[4] Presumably Cutter was speaking of venereal disease, one of the afflictions that drew many to the thermal springs. In spite of Cutter's claims, of course, Hot Springs would continue to be a mecca for gambling and other vices for decades to come.

The highest aim in life should be, to relieve suffering humanity; to bring sunshine where there is darkness, and to cause health and joy where sickness and sorrow reigns.

CONSULTATION FREE

DR. EDMUND S. LEFLER
D. M. T. D. C.

A growing number of physicians were coming to Hot Springs in the 1880s to meet the demand and to earn a living. Many advertised, as did Dr. Edmund S. Lefler, by offering a free consultation. He worked from three rooms of the Rector Hotel on Central Avenue. The back of his card announced, "Nervous and Chronic Diseases a Specialty." He often prescribed a course of baths as part of a patient's treatment.

Gambling Shows Its Ugly Side

Cutter's efforts to reassure would-be Hot Springs visitors that the gambling had been cleaned up had some background story. Gambling-related violence had played out on Central Avenue in a series of incidents in the early 1880s, and in the summer of 1882 Charles Matthews, editor of the *Hot Springs Daily Hornet,* attacked both the illegal gambling and Mayor T. F. Linde for doing nothing to stop it. Linde, a dentist who served as both mayor and police judge at the time,

The bridging over of Hot Springs Creek with a stone arch in 1884 was the largest public works project in Hot Springs history. What had before been an eyesore, at times an open sewer, became a concealed storm drain and made possible a wider Central Avenue. With Hot Springs Creek buried beneath the street, a more orderly look was coming to Central Avenue in the 1880s. Larger, more modern bathhouses took advantage of the wider avenue. The wooden-frame bathhouses lined the right side of the dirt street, and the business district the left. The owners of the town's bathhouses formed the Hot Springs Bathhouse Association in 1882 with the avowed goal of stopping "drumming," or the hustlers who met patrons at the depot attempting to direct them to a particular business in exchange for a commission. The group became instead more of a price-fixing monopoly.

was so irate over a recent editorial that, upon meeting Matthews on the street, he pulled his pistol and began firing, inflicting three nonfatal wounds on the newspaper man and wounding both a peddler and a city councilman who happened to be in the line of fire. Incredibly, the mayor was neither charged nor removed from office in an era that found a "wild west" air about Hot Springs.

Recovering from his wounds, Matthews with renewed vengeance

took up his pen again. In addition to targeting the mayor, he launched printed salvos against prominent citizens with ties to the gambling business, most notably the wealthy and powerful Samuel L. Fordyce who owned an interest in the Arlington Hotel and its own self-contained gambling club. Matthews linked Fordyce, his partner D. C. Rugg, and the town's notorious gambler Frank Flynn, labeling them in his paper the "Arlington Gang." Flynn operated a Central Avenue gambling house of questionable honesty called The Office Saloon.

Fordyce, carrying a heavy cane and a gun, confronted Matthews on Central Avenue near the DeSoto Valley Spring. Irate over the editorial, Fordyce struck Matthews with his cane, and Matthews pulled his pistol in self-defense, firing but missing. Matthews had retreated into the street as Fordyce's partner D. C. Rugg appeared with his own gun drawn; Rugg took a bullet in the leg from the newspaperman's gun. Down and in pain, Rugg yelled, "He got me. Run him down, boys. Run him down." Matthews was already down in the street, wounded at least once, when gambler Flynn, the third member of the so-called Arlington Gang, appeared and fired a final fatal shot at Matthews. The editor dropped into the mud of Central Avenue. Fordyce, Flynn, and Rugg were all charged with manslaughter; Flynn and Rugg were acquitted while Fordyce was fined two hundred dollars for starting what turned out to be a fatal confrontation by attacking Matthews with his cane. Frank Flynn, a Canadian by birth, had arrived in Hot Springs after the Civil War and would again make headlines for gambling-related violence in September 1884, by which time his hold on the games of chance in the "Spa City" had earned him the title "Boss Gambler." Two years after the slaying of Matthews, Flynn owned outright, or allowed to operate under his blessing, virtually all of the half dozen major gambling houses on Central Avenue.

Jim Lane, a gambling entrepreneur from Illinois, came to Hot Springs around 1880 and opened two high-end gambling halls, The Palace and The Monarch. Lane refused to align with Frank Flynn—nor did he pay a percentage to Flynn for the right to operate his business. Flynn, lest he appear weak, decided Lane must go, and with a mob backing him he attacked and wrecked The Palace. One of Lane's card dealers killed one of Flynn's thugs, but it was too much for Lane and he fled the city. Flynn was firmly in control of all of Hot Springs' gambling once again.

The Palace Bathhouse was described in one tourist guide in 1884 as the finest bathing establishment in the nation. It opened in 1880, the work of Samuel Fordyce and Charles Maurice who would later compete for the upscale bathing trade. Per *Cutters Guide to Hot Springs,* it was "one of the best, if not the best, bathing establishments in the world" with twenty-four enameled tubs imported from Europe. A soak in 1884 cost thirty cents or $6.30 for a course of twenty-one baths. The price was the maximum charge allowed by the secretary of the interior who set price caps on the houses sitting on leased federal land.[5] The site is today occupied by the Fordyce Bathhouse, which houses the visitors center for Hot Springs National Park. *Courtesy of Arkansas History Commission*

However, Jim Lane would be heard from yet again, having gone to New Orleans to lick his wounds. While in the Crescent City he met former Confederate major S. A. Doran, who upon hearing what had happened to Lane at Frank Flynn's hands decided to go to Hot Springs and challenge the gambling kingpin. Doran arrived in Hot Springs during the winter of 1883 and proceeded to reopen The Palace; he blatantly enraged Flynn by refusing to join his gambling ring, declaring his independence from Boss Gambler. Flynn began to recruit gunmen from Texas and the Oklahoma territories, planning to go to war if necessary to push Doran out and regain dominance. Doran, a war

Samuel W. Fordyce, a former Union Army officer from Ohio, settled in Hot Springs in 1876. With his wealth from railroads and other ventures he partnered to build the Arlington Hotel. John Fordyce was a man with a temper, as a local newspaper editor would discover when Fordyce attacked the critical journalist with his cane.

veteran not as easily intimidated as Mr. Lane, imported his own army of gunfighters. Hot Springs soon took on the air of an armed camp, much like the wild west depicted in contemporary dime novels.

The armed stalemate would prove bad for business in all the gambling houses, as too many people were afraid of the gunfighters pacing the streets and gaming halls and hence were unwilling to patronize the houses. Something had to give. Shots were fired in the street, and Major Doran got the message that Flynn was calling him out into Central Avenue for a shootout to settle the standoff. In the salvo of shots between the two men, Flynn was slightly wounded while Doran was unhurt. Doran swore Flynn had been wearing some sort of bulletproof vest of armor.

The first of what would be three Arlington hotels in Hot Springs opened in 1875. The hotel was considered from its opening to be the town's finest, with quoted rates from seventeen to twenty-one dollars per week. S. H. Stitt was proud of his hotel, adding an extension in 1886 with a 60' × 120' dining room, a gentlemen's reading room, and a ladies' parlor, lest a guest wish not to sit on the eight-foot front porch on Central Avenue near Fountain Street. It anchored the north end of Bathhouse Row.[6] *Courtesy of Arkansas History Commission*

Flynn's plan was to rent a room at the Arlington Hotel overlooking the front of Doran's gambling hall and gun him down when he emerged from the building. This less-than-sporting plan, even in a gambling town, alienated the locals who previously had favored Flynn over the outsider Doran. On a midwinter morning with a cold drizzle falling, Frank Flynn and his brothers Jack and Billy were in a hack at the south end of bathhouse row when a half dozen of Doran's men opened fire, killing Jack Flynn and the driver. Billy Flynn collapsed on the boardwalk near the Rammelsburg bathhouse with a load of buckshot in his stomach. Stray bullets killed or wounded several bystanders before the chief of police Tom Toller arrived to restore order.[7]

The city had finally had enough; its economy was suffering, and visitors were staying away. A committee of twelve was formed, backed by the police and armed citizens. This panel forced a long list of gamblers, including the surviving Flynn brothers and Major Doran, to

Aging and infirmed with battle wounds, soldiers of both the Union and Confederate armies were making treks to Hot Springs in the 1880s but finding little access to health-care while seeking the thermal baths. Local physician A. S. Garnett lobbied visiting Illinois senator and former Union general John H. Logan for help. Logan, feeling the baths had improved his health, pledged to return to Washington and secure the funding for what became the Army and Navy Hospital, one of the most prominent landmarks in Hot Springs when completed in 1887. The new military hospital, erected at a cost of $200,000, formally opened in January 1887 and two days later admitted its first patient, former Confederate captain L. Gaines of Tennessee.

pack up and move on, escorting them to the train depot and forcing them out of Hot Springs. The gambling halls were allowed to reopen under new managers, for the city's take of the proceeds was a vital source of revenue. As a postscript, Major Doran, while he escaped Hot Springs with his life, would be shot to death in a saloon in Fort Smith, Arkansas, two years later.

The 1880s drew to a close, ending a decade that had seen unparalleled growth in the city of Hot Springs, including some fine hotels, grand homes, sturdy bathhouses, a new government hospital, and a renewed concern for the less fortunate, all wrapped around the anticipation of a bright future. The decade to come would be all that was hoped for, and more besides.

With 520 rooms the grand Eastman Hotel claimed the title of Hot Springs largest when it opened in 1890. The hotel was the inspiration of the wealthy George Eastman who already owned the Hale Bathhouse. The main halls were twelve feet wide, extending the length of the building and forming a promenade 675 feet long. Aside from its sheer size the biggest draw was the observatory tower that rose some 200 feet, affording a stunning view of the city and surrounding mountains.

CHAPTER FIVE

Victorian Splendor
1890–1900

When the 1890s rolled in, Hot Springs was well on its way to becoming one of the best-known spa resorts in the nation, earning comparison to the fine spas of Europe and labeled by some as the "American Carlsbad," after the famed German resort. It became easier to reach the city in 1890 when Diamond Joe Reynolds finally widened his tracks from Malvern to allow full-size trains to make the journey—and the private rail cars of the wealthy soon followed.

In a May 18, 1893, story touting the thermal waters, the *Hot Springs Daily News* proclaimed in bold headlines that Hot Springs was the world's greatest health resort, "A Boon To Suffering Humanity Wrought by the Hand of God"; "It is to The Earth's Afflicted What the Brazen Serpent Was to the Israelites"; "And yet, Like the Unbelieving Jews, Thousands Die Because They Will Not Come and Be Healed." The paper audaciously compared the suffering of those who refused to come to Hot Springs to the Israelites who refused to look upon the image of the bronze serpent Moses had erected, thus dying rather than being healed of their snake bites. "The people of the earth today are among the snakes. The deadly adders of disease are striking poisonous fangs into thousands everywhere. They are dying right and left. Death knells commingle with wedding bells in every village and hamlet. Hot Springs, a God-endowed Bethesda, is to those people what the brazen serpent is alleged to have been to the Israelites . . . if they will but come, and not delay too long."[1]

The peak season for visitors to Hot Springs was from January to June, allowing the high-society people of the cold northern cities a chance to escape the winter, enjoy the spa, and return home before the oppressive southern summer took hold. *Ye Hot Springs, Arkansas,*

Picture Booke, published in 1894, summed up the feeling conveyed about the city: "There is not an hour in the twenty-four that one cannot be entertained here to the full limit of his tastes, from a church fair to a cake walk, a milkmaid's convention to a Y.M.C.A. lecture or a good sermon to a jack-pot or a prize fight."[2]

Violence in the Last Year of the Century

Before the 1890s closed into history, a new chapter would be written in the annals of gambling and violence in the city. Hot Springs' love/hate relationship with gambling had been in constant play since the gun battles of Flynn and Doran in 1884. One faction of the town thought gambling was good and even essential for the economy, while another thought it was a stain on the Spa City's image, for the lure of the hot waters should have been enough without gambling. A mayor was elected every two years—and the mayor got to pick the police chief— and it was this pair of leaders that tended to determine the extent of gambling in the resort. When the independent candidate William Gordon defeated the incumbent mayor in 1897, he reached into the town's past and appointed Tom Toler as chief of police. Toler had been chief during the Flynn and Doran battles and had helped run them out of town. The forty-five-year-old Toler soon split with the new mayor on gambling by favoring a wide-open town that supported gambling. The mayor regretted his choice and sought to fire Toler but was over- ruled by the town council. By the 1899 election, a young businessman named George Belding was running for mayor and was aligning himself with Garland County sheriff Robert Williams by promising to appoint the sheriff's brother, Coffee Williams, as chief of police if elected. This did not sit well with Tom Toler, as the current chief.

Toler was popular in Hot Springs. He ran his ten-man force by collecting just enough fines to support their salaries, but he did not crack down on the gambling and prostitution that many felt drew visitors and money to Hot Springs. Just as Toler's men were supportive of their chief so also were the deputies on the force of Sheriff Williams supportive of their boss's candidate. It seemed that a clash of some sort was almost inevitable, but few anticipated the violence that ensued.

On the morning of March 16, 1899, Chief Toler organized a meet-

As the owners of the Arlington Hotel, Samuel Fordyce and his investors saw the competition the grander Eastman and Park hotels were bringing to Hot Springs, and they knew their hotel could not compete. They replaced it with a new Arlington, a red brick Moorish-style hotel spanning 650 feet of Central Avenue in 1893. At a cost of $500,000 and a capacity of 500 guests, the hotel had an immediate impact. The *Chicago 400 Journal of Topics,* which catered to the wealthy of northern cities, compared the new Arlington with Chicago's Palmer House hotel, saying that if you "dropped anchor in this hub of Hot Springs for a half hour, you will be certain to see everybody who is anybody."[3] Of the Arlington *Ye Hot Springs, Arkansas, Picture Booke,* published in 1894, stated that at the hotel "nothing that contributes to convenience and comfort has been omitted," including elevators, a barber shop, a Western Union, and two hot springs on the mountainside behind the hotel. "Invalid guests can be wheeled in rolling chairs supplied by the hotel from any chamber in the hotel to the baths." A grand staircase greeted arriving guests at the new Arlington Hotel in 1893.[4]

ing in his office with C. W. Fry, the independent mayoral candidate. The men made a pact that if Fry won the election, Toler would keep his job along with the ten men in his department. Someone phoned Sheriff Williams to inform him of the meeting, and in anger he stormed downtown to the Klondike Saloon. After a ranting conversation about people plotting against him, Williams swaggered down Central Avenue where he met up with police sergeant Tom Goslee and targeted the Toler employee with his wrath. Armed with only a two-shot derringer, Sergeant Goslee sought to disengage from the confrontation.

Those seeking more modest prices than hotels like the Arlington might have found their way to the wooden-framed Imperial Hotel at the corner of Cottage and Spring streets. A block off Central Avenue, the advertised room rate in the early years of the twentieth century was a dollar a day. What might have been a full house of guests posed at the front porch around 1910. The hotel was razed many years ago; the site today is home to the *Hot Springs Sentinel Record*.

Imperial Bath House, Hot Springs, Ark.

The Imperial Bathhouse rose in 1894 below the Army and Navy Hospital facing Reserve Avenue, just off Central across from the massive Eastman Hotel. Its bathing tubs were imported from England, covered in what one tour guide described as "Royal porcelain." The grand building was razed in the 1930s to make way for a new park headquarters.

7446. Entrance to Government Reservation, Hot Springs, Ark.

The centerpiece for the U.S. Government Reservation in Hot Springs was a grand staircase leading to a marble bandstand on the hill behind the Maurice and Palace bathhouses. The Greek revival structure was the accomplishment of U.S. War Department designer Lt. Robert Stevens, who developed the first real master plan for the reservation. The bandstand was removed many years ago, but the steps remain.

opposite page and above: The Rockafellow Bathhouse at the corner of Central and Park avenues provided both robes and spittoons to its bathers. The bathhouse is seen right of center in this photograph looking down the path of new streetcar tracks approaching from Whittington Avenue. Named for a nineteenth-century businessman and pharmacist, the Rockafellow, which curved around the corner of Park Avenue at Central, was razed in the 1960s. The site today is but a parking lot. *Courtesy of Garland County Historical Society*

At that point, Sheriff Williams's son came out of the City Hall Saloon and handed his father a .44 revolver. The bullets started flying, four-teen shots in all. Due perhaps to poor marksmanship, nobody was injured, and Sergeant Goslee was rescued by his boss, Chief Toler, from the hotel in which he had taken refuge.

The city fathers were irate about a gun battle having again erupted on Central Avenue, and Sheriff Williams and Chief Toler were told flatly to end the conflict. A meeting between them was planned for the same evening at Toler's house. The supporters of both camps moved around the city that evening, all heavily armed, and several ended up in a saloon called Lemp's Beer Depot. Deputy sheriff Ed Spear exchanged angry words with bartender Louis Hinkle, whose brother was on Chief Toler's force; this was the spark that ended the lives of five men and made

Hot Springs police chief Tom Toler, wearing the derby hat in the center, served at the pleasure of the mayor, and by extension so did the entire police force. Toler died on the streets of Hot Springs in one of the bloodiest battles in the city's history, with gambling as the root cause. *Courtesy of Garland County Historical Society*

headlines as far away as New York City. The brawny bartender slashed Deputy Spear's throat with a knife, whereupon the profusely bleeding Spear twisted free and shot the bartender through the throat, the bullet exiting his ear. Coffee Williams, the sheriff's brother and the aspiring police chief candidate, pulled his pistol and shot bartender Hinkle in the chest. More shooting erupted outside in the street. Sergeant Goslee, who had escaped the fourteen shots earlier in the day, was wounded and then killed by a second shot from Coffee Williams, who had rushed out of Lemp's Beer Depot after shooting the bartender.

Shots from the arriving policemen hit Sheriff Williams's son Johnny in the head as he emerged from the nearby Klondike Saloon. Meanwhile Chief Toler found himself in a swarm of bullets fired by Coffee Williams and the bleeding Ed Spears, victim of the bartender's knife. Trying to hide and return fire from the cover of a nearby freight wagon, Chief

Hot Springs had its own version of Coney Island by the 1890s in Whittington Park, set on eleven acres at the upper end of Whittington Avenue. Home of the state's largest roller coaster, the park hosted prize fights, one attended in 1896 by Theodore Roosevelt, a police commissioner from New York City who would become president five years later. The park hosted political rallies and served as a training site for professional baseball teams like the Pittsburg Pirates. The park closed in 1961. *Courtesy of Garland County Historical Society*

Toler was hit in the back of the head, dying quickly in the dirt of Central Avenue. But the killing was not over yet. Police detective Jim Hart, who was on duty at the train depot, arrived after the shooting was over and tried to sort out what had happened; he found his chief dead in the street among the other victims. Hart came face-to-face with Sheriff Williams, who was distraught at thinking that his son Johnny was dead. Indeed, the young man was still alive at that point but died later that evening of his wounds. Williams grabbed detective Hart by the collar, yelling,

Aside from exciting roller coaster rides, Whittington Park offered more peaceful pastimes such as the picnic this group was photographed having around 1900.

As the new century loomed Hot Springs was still a town of horses and dirt streets, looking more like a wild-west town than the world-class resort it billed itself to be.
Courtesy of Garland County Historical Society

The first automobile in Hot Springs was the Locomobile pictured here from 1899. Miss Emma Whittington of the prominent pioneer family ordered the steam-powered automobile and had it shipped in by train. Its presence on the streets of the city was short lived, for one day someone forgot to turn off the steam and the car's boiler erupted, destroying the vehicle.[6] *Courtesy of Garland County Historical Society*

"Here is another one of those sons-of-bitches," then pulled his revolver, put it into Hart's face, and blew off the top of the man's head. To add further damage, one of Sheriff Williams's deputies fired two more shots into the detective's body.

Chief Toler's wife reportedly arrived on the scene, having been summoned by friends, to find her husband's bloody body lying in the street. As reported in the *Hot Springs Daily News,* "She seemed cool and determined to avenge his death. . . . She is said to have displayed a revolver from beneath her cloak and asked bystanders to show her the man who killed Mr. Toler."[5] Bystanders quickly shepherded her away before she could add to the toll of violence. Ed Spear finally settled down and lived for many years in Hot Springs, until his death in 1950, a half century after participating in the bloodiest gun battle in the city's history.

As the year 1900 approached, Hot Springs was indeed ready for a new century, hoping it would be both prosperous and peaceful.

When the twentieth century opened a heavy snow had fallen on Bathhouse Row. The city was preparing for its high season that would run until the heat of summer drove the hordes of visitors back north. *Courtesy of Garland County Historical Society*

CHAPTER SIX

Opulence, Glamour, and Disaster
1900–1910

The new century opened with a population of ten thousand in Hot Springs, where little more than a century earlier only the moccasin-clad feet of Indians had walked.[1] The city was served by a second railroad in 1900, when Diamond Joe Reynolds's monopoly was broken by Col. Sam Fordyce who brought the tracks of the Little Rock and Hot Springs Western Railroad into the city. The city now had six public schools—four for white children and two for black children—along with churches of all major denominations and three hospitals. Most importantly to the city fathers, the violent shootout of 1899 between opposing factions of law enforcement officers, which had made vivid headlines nationwide, seemed not to have impeded the flow of visitors to the city.

The February 1901 edition of the *Herald,* in the midst of profiles of hotels and bathhouses, served up testimonials from out-of-state patrons as to the healing properties of the thermal waters. Mrs. P. T. Teter of West Virginia wrote,

> I had a most severe attack of rheumatism, which lasted five months before I decided to come to Hot Springs. I could not rest without the aid of opiates, and I literally had to be carried to the hotel on a cot, having suffered most excruciating pain on the way here. Every movement of the car made me scream. My feet were drawn up so that I was unable to get them to the floor and could not make any use of them. My cure was almost marvelous from the very beginning. After the first bath I slept for the first time in five weeks without opiates. On the fifth day I was able to walk alone, and on the thirteenth day I climbed two flights of stairs without assistance, as well, in fact, as I ever could, and I gained six pounds in that time.[2]

South of Bathhouse Row, the working part of Central Avenue opened up to a series of small shops and rooming houses. The New Oklahoman "Furnished Rooms" is to the left above the blurred horse.

The wealthy elite of Chicago had a love affair with Hot Springs for much of the early part of the twentieth century, as displayed in the February 1903 edition of the fashionable Chicago magazine *The 400*. A reporter for the magazine came to Hot Springs in the winter of 1902 to do a feature on what the city would be like as the 1903 high season got underway. "Alighting from the trains, the resorters are confronted with new buildings and roofs in every direction, the musical sounds of the busy hammer and saw, the freshly painted mammoth hotels and cozy clubhouses, newly macadamized streets and cemented promenades, and a general atmosphere of great expectations." The journalist forecast that soon Hot Springs would be on par with world-renowned resorts like Monte Carlo and Naples. Followed along on the implications of this dream, the writer rhapsodized, "I also perceive a Chicago–Hot Springs air line [of] macadamized highway, lined with meteoric automobiles ribbonning off the seven hundred and fifty miles in a thousand or less minutes. The perspective is almost delirious."[3]

Professional baseball teams, like the Brooklyn Dodgers seen here in 1912, did their winter training in Hot Springs for the early part of the twentieth century. The Chicago Cubs were first, joined by the Pittsburg Pirates in 1901. The Boston Red Sox, along with budding star Babe Ruth, soon followed. Ordinary visitors often wrote postcards home talking about hotel-lobby sightings of the athletes.

The almost constant strife between those supporting the open-city concept toward gambling and other vices and those closed-city advocates who opposed the "sins" had gone on in Hot Springs for many years. An editorial on June 9, 1903, in the *Daily News* was penned by one who was tired of the bickering. Headlined "GONE TO EXTREMES," the piece stated that "Hot Springs is afflicted with excesses. It's irritated with extremes. Mass meetings are decrying lawlessness on the one hand, and in the other direction fanaticism under the guise of religion runs rampant and unrestrained. Between the two revolting extremes decent and intelligent people are annoyed, disgusted and humiliated. Whether the open operations of the sporting

"Tally Ho" parties were popular with many visitors. Twenty or more people would ride one of the large coaches over the mountain trails around the city.

The Majestic Hotel opened on Park Avenue in 1902, just down from the intersection with Central. The Majestic was built on the Park Avenue site occupied by the landmark Avenue Hotel. Charles Cutter's souvenir guide in 1904 said of the hotel, "Hot and cold water in every room . . . Thirty-six suites with private toilets . . . Six public toilets on every floor."[4] Each of the four stories was connected to the mountainside behind the hotel by an iron pedestrian bridge. The St. Charles Hotel is visible further down Park Avenue. The Majestic closed in 2006; efforts to restore it as housing for the disabled were envisioned, but funding issues left the grand hotel vacant.

The Hot Springs Alligator Farm, opened in 1902, still operates today, though visitors can no longer pose atop a stuffed alligator. H. I. Campbell stocked his facility on Whittington Avenue with fifty Florida alligators and even built slides the alligators could ride down while tourists watched. The highlight came at feeding time, especially when the attendants tossed the alligators a live chicken.

[gambling] fraternity is more annoying to the intelligent citizen and visitor than the public rantings of the street corner religious loonies is a question."[5] The paper's position probably reflected the "live and let live" attitude of the majority of the population, which allowed gambling to continue for decades to come.

In the first decade of a new century, the Hot Springs clergy were prone to voice dismay about the perceived sinfulness of the open city Hot Springs had become. Clergy members put their concerns in print to the reservation superintendent, writing, "There is in Hot Springs a state of moral degradation in the form of gambling, wide openness and general sporting, to the extent of twenty-seven regular gambling houses from which fines are collected by city authorities; six pool rooms, two

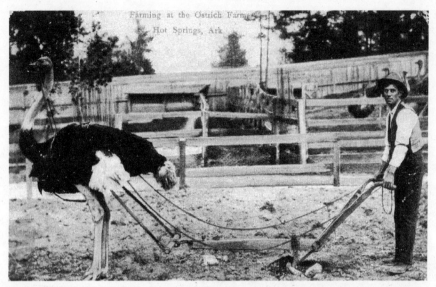

The Ostrich Farm was a Hot Springs attraction for a half century, drawing tourists to see things like one of the giant birds pulling a plow. Thomas Cockburn imported three hundred of the giant birds to create the attraction in 1900 on Whittington Avenue. Visitors delighted in seeing such birds as Black Diamond, which stood almost nine feet tall. The attraction closed in the 1950s.

The Iron Mountain Railroad brought full-size trains to the city by 1900, using this depot within sight of the Park Hotel to the left. Coaches from the Park and other high-end hotels would meet guests at the depot upon their arrival. The depot and the grand hotel would both be lost to fire in September 1913.

Passengers arriving at the Iron Mountain depot would have gotten a sight of the hot water even before alighting from the train. Steam may be seen rising from Hot Springs Creek that emerged near the depot from the underground tunnel that drained the hot water from beneath Bathhouse Row.

race tracks; non-Sunday observance, and from 300 to 1,500 scarlet women, and in consequence of which lawlessness and disregard for the name of our fair city, there is very little protection for the visitor against the ravages of such demoralizing influences." The churchmen's elegant pleas fell upon deaf ears within the city's elected leadership, and the reservation superintendent had no power to act outside the federal land and the leased bathhouses located on that property.[6]

Prostitution at the time was treated by city officials much like gambling, as a necessary part of the economy that helped city coffers with "fine" revenue. Police judge Vernal Ledgerwood was distressed to learn after some time in office that his salary and expenses were appropriated by the town council from the fines levied against the prostitution trade. So troubled was Ledgerwood over this that he informed the mayor that he must find another funding source or "I'm going to let the women go without fines."[10]

Hot Springs' love/hate relationship with sin would be waged for decades yet to come.

The New Hot Springs Bath House, Hot Springs, Ark.

Newest and Largest Bath House in the City.
Elegantly Furnished Rooms in Connection.

A Mr. A. C. McDonald visited Hot Springs in July 1908, lodging at Jacob's House, a boarding house on Fountain Street where he got his meals for twenty cents, or twenty-one meals for three dollars, as he got his card punched at meal time. He took his baths at the Hot Springs Bathhouse, located just north of the Arlington Hotel, getting twenty-one baths for seven dollars.

GOOD FOR 21 MEALS
—AT—
JACOBS HOUSE
JACOBS & PIKE, Propr's
PRICE $3.00
SINGLE MEALS 20c   5 FOUNTAIN ST.

NEW HOT SPRINGS BATH HOUSE
Hot Springs, Ark.   July 26-08
M A. C. McDonald
Attendant Andrew
PRICE $7.00
21st Bath Complimentary
No. 3762

To improve business Hot Springs and its bathhouses began to market to women, making claims that the bath treatments could restore youthful appearance. The railroads cooperated, making travel to the city attractive to women like this group around 1905.

$25 REWARD

For the arrest of one W. R. Gannon, weigh~~s about~~ ~~150~~ pounds, height about 5 feet 8½ to 9 inches, slightly stoops ~~in walking~~, dark hair, bad teeth, eyebrows connect, shoes No. 8, hat 7⅛, incessant cigarette smoker, frequents saloons, low dives and gambling halls, writes a good hand, is a fair painter, had on light suit of clothes with Morris Bros' tag in coat collar and straw hat when last seen. Wanted for embezzlement. Arrest and notify by wire.

Age 33 to 35
Irish American

A. R. ANDERSON,
SHERIFF HARRIS COUNTY,
HOUSTON, TEXAS

Hot Springs' reputation for drawing con artists and others fleeing the law often prompted police agencies around the nation to send notices of various wanted felons to the Hot Springs police chief.

Hot Spring Feb 14 – 07

Arkansas State Fair.—Oak Lawn Race Track, Hot Springs, Ark.

This is the place where people gets broke it is as bad as Monte Carlo Auntie Ceruha

"This is the place where people gets broke, it is as bad as Monte Carlo," reads the card, suggesting its mailer had not fared well at the horse races at the new Oaklawn Park in 1907. Oaklawn was created to compete with an earlier track, Essex Park, which was further from the tourist portion of the city. The state's ban on wagering on the horses, enacted in 1907, caused the demise of Essex Park and shuttered Oaklawn for a decade.

In 1907 the nurses and nuns from St. Joseph's Infirmary stationed their ambulance at Oaklawn to be on hand for any injured or sick. It was perhaps part mission and part prominent advertising of the Catholic healthcare institution. The Sisters of Mercy had first opened an infirmary in 1888 and in 1903 opened a hospital on Whittington Avenue. More than a century later St. Joseph's, in a sprawling modern facility on the edge of the city, continues to serve Hot Springs.

"Greetings from the City of Invalids and Cripples" summed up the view of one visitor in 1903, a reminder that it was the promise of restored health that was bringing thousands of visitors to Hot Springs.

Be Sure to Visit the Great Steel

OBSERVATION TOWER

ON HOT SPRINGS MOUNTAIN

¶ Its Upper Floor Affords the Finest View Ever Obtained of Central Arkansas. ::

¶ Built Entirely of Steel, it is Strong, Safe and Beautiful. 165 Feet High. :: ::

¶ Fine Elevator Service. Easy Grade Stairway

The second tower to crown Hot Springs Mountain was erected in 1906, its 165 feet dwarfing the wooden 75-foot tower it replaced. The Texas Bridge Company of Dallas leased the land atop Hot Springs Mountain and spent $20,000 to build the tower and its 166-square-foot observation platform. The tower came down in 1971 to be replaced a few years later by yet a third tower.[8]

Hot Springs had been spared a serious fire for a decade, but its luck ran out in 1905. Sparks ignited in the Grand Hotel and soon swept over south Hot Springs. Much of the town's Victorian heritage was lost, including this grand building that housed the post office. The *Sentinel Record* said, "It was a morning of horror—of many horrors. One horror followed fast on the heels of another. It was a morning of ghastly scenes that will live in memory until the day of final accounts."[7] *Courtesy of Garland County Historical Society*

The streetcar barn where the cars were stored and repaired was located on Park Avenue, where most of the drivers posed here around 1905. *Courtesy of Garland County Historical Society*

The Strobel airship thrilled Hot Springs in 1909 as it soared over the city, but travel in such vessels would not prove practical over time. As reported by the *Sentinel Record* the seventy-five-foot dirigible soared "with the grace of a bird of passage, lofted from the center of the entertainment arena at Oaklawn, soared along the feathered edge of the white tinged clouds of the morning sky, shifted to the downtown district and took a whirl around the Eastman tower, . . . glided aloof from the green pines of Hot Springs Mountain to a circle around the great steel observatory."[9] *Courtesy of Garland County Historical Society*

A number of small
hotels were lost in the
1905 fire including the
Hotel Moody, which
would be the first of
three Moody Hotels to
be lost by fire over the
next seventy years.
*Courtesy of Garland
County Historical
Society*

The aftermath of the greatest fire Arkansas had yet seen brought out gawkers and photographers surveying the vast spread of the damage. The Garland County courthouse
(along with many of its records), the Jewish synagogue, and even the home of the sheriff
were all lost. Some of the public records in the courthouse were rescued when Sheriff
Bob Williams deployed prisoners from the jail to move out as many files as they could
carry ahead of the advancing flames. *Courtesy of Garland County Historical Society*

CHAPTER SEVEN

Prohibition, War, and a Great Inferno
1910–1920

As 1910 rolled around, Hot Springs counted a population of 14,434, representing a 45 percent increase over the 1900 census count.[1] The bathing industry continued to prosper, and expectations were high for the new decade, but a drag on the local economy continued in the statewide ban on legal gambling enacted in 1907 that specified no wagering on horse races. The Missouri Pacific Iron Mountain Railroad's 1910 guidebook for Hot Springs tried to compensate for these missing entertainments by broadly praising the waters: "It is well to have a Mecca somewhere on earth for the cure of those who suffer cutaneously and viscerally; whose outer envelope may be disorganized and disfigured, and whose larger internal vessels may refuse their function in a trying or even dangerous way. It is well, we repeat, to have found such a place, such a body of water rushing from the generous centers of nature."

Another Violent Episode

While 1910 carried Hot Springs to high excitement with its many wealthy and famous visitors, it also saw a return to the angst of gun violence that the city hoped had faded into history. The violence came on August 17, 1910, from two sets of brothers: the newly re-elected Garland County sheriff Jake Houpt and his chief deputy and brother, Sid, and the brothers George and Oscar Chitwood. The Houpts had been asked by the Clark County sheriff in Arkadelphia to look for the Chitwoods, two alleged horse thieves who were known to have fled to Hot Springs. Deputy Sid Houpt happened upon the two men as they were saddling up their horses to ride out of town. Without giving the men reasons, Deputy Houpt persuaded them to come to the sheriff's

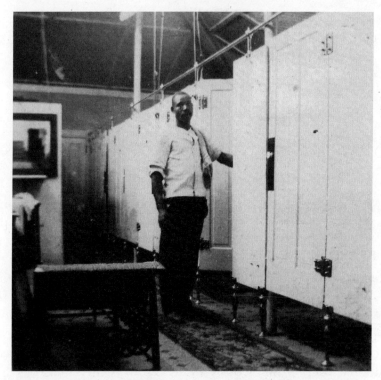

In the early 1900s the attendants in the bathhouses, working hard in sweltering conditions, were almost exclusively black men and women. Said Superintendent Eisele's 1903 report, "All bath house attendants bathe their persons every day. When they report for duty they disrobe and put on a bathing suit of white duck trousers and a thin gauze undershirt; their duties require them to work in a temperature of 95 to100 degrees. Being a hazardous business and destructive of health, white men shun this work, and it follows that the Negro is the natural bath attendant."[2] *Courtesy of Garland County Historical Society*

office. Upon arriving in front of the sheriff's desk the men found themselves served with warrants for their arrest on the horse-theft charges. After that, things failed to go at all like the Houpts had envisioned, for the two outlaw brothers pulled pistols on the lawmen and ran from the courthouse office, with the Houpts in pursuit and bullets flying in both directions. The Chitwoods managed to reach their tethered horses and soon raced onto Ouachita Avenue, but the horses' shod hooves slid from beneath them on the slick railroad tracks that crossed the streets.

Sid Houpt fired his last shot, striking Oscar Chitwood's elbow, then

Government
Free Bath House,
Hot Springs, Ark.

For those who could not pay for their bath, Congress mandated facilities for the indigent, which gave rise to the government's opening of a free bathhouse in 1891. By 1910 inspectors demanded a new facility: "It is in bad repair, dingy and uninviting looking, it is over crowded, for the indigent have not been slow to take advantage of the paternal goodness of the Government. They troop in by scores, both sexes and all colors, afflicted with all kinds of diseases. Some days there are 800 taking the baths. The dressing and cooling rooms are foul, infested with vermin and crowded with a horde of people, some with open ulcers. The atmosphere is indescribable."[3] A new government free bath house finally opened in 1921.

had to race back into the courthouse for a new box of bullets. Sheriff Houpt continued the pursuit alone, watching George Chitwood take cover behind a streetcar, both men preparing to open fire. The sheriff was a split second slower, but as a bullet pierced his side he still made his own shot as he was falling and struck Chitwood. Sid Houpt returned in time to see his brother and the assailant both down in the street. The deputy fired a bullet from his now reloaded revolver into the man who had just shot his brother and then leaped aboard a buggy in pursuit of the other Chitwood brother. Oscar was fleeing on horseback, and the buggy lost the race. Chitwood disappeared into the countryside.

The wound in Sheriff Houpt's side would prove fatal after two agonizing days. His killer, George Chitwood, had died on Ouachita Avenue, and his brother Oscar was captured before the sheriff's

Although black residents had long been the labor mainstay of the bathing business, their use of the facilities as patrons was seldom allowed. The Crystal Bathhouse was the first to be built exclusively for black residents and visitors. It opened in 1904 at 415 Malvern Avenue. Owned by African Americans M. H. Jodd and A. R. Aldrich, the lease was transferred to the Knights of Pythias in 1908. The Crystal would be destroyed in the great fire of 1913, leaving blacks for a time with access only to the thermal baths at the government's indigent facility.

In 1914 the Knights of Pythias, having lost the Crystal in the previous year's fire, erected the Pythian Bathhouse on the same Malvern Avenue site. African American W. T. Bailey, an architect at the Tuskeegee Institute, designed the building. The bathhouse served black residents and visitors profitably through desegregation in 1965 but closed in 1974. Today the site is a parking lot for the Austin Hotel.

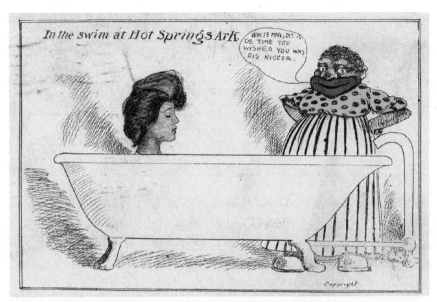

Today such a postcard would be seen as blatantly racist, but this one of a black bath attendant, mailed in 1909, was considered humorous for tourists to send home. The hardworking attendants who supported the bathhouse economy got little respect even from reservation superintendent Eisele's 1903 report: "So far as their work is concerned it compares favorably with other laborers of this grade of intelligence."[4]

In 1914 William Maurice opened what would be for a short time the finest bathhouse in Hot Springs on the same site as his older wooden bathhouse. The Cutter guidebook gave a glowing review: "250 large, enamel steel dressing rooms for men, 50 for women . . . Two large gymnasiums, complete massage and Electric Departments, Sitz and Nauheim Baths, Manicure, Hair Dressing, Chiropody, and Mercurial Rubbing Department." The latter technique was most often used for treating syphilis. A course of twenty-one baths was quoted at thirteen dollars when the facility opened.[5] *Courtesy of Arkansas History Commission*

William Maurice's name was attached to the spring behind his bathhouse that fed the tubs. Its location beneath the grand entrance to the federal reservation made it a popular photograph spot.

The owners of the stately new Buckstaff Bathhouse sought and received federal permission to use only white attendants, a fact that was advertised on postcards. At a cost of $125,000 the Buckstaff opened not long after the Maurice, on the site of the former Rammelsberg Bathhouse. Charles Cutter approved, touting the "seamless marble as disease free. . . . Nowhere can the prolific and adaptive germ get a lodging place to start a family . . . Splendid mahogany doors lead to the baths." Hot Springs superintendent Harry Meyers wrote the secretary of the interior that the Buckstaff resembled "the Irish House of Parliament or the White House."[6]

WILLIAM G. MAURICE.

May you live as long as you like.
And have what you like as long as you live.

William Maurice first visited Hot Springs in 1870. He would return to build the grandest bathhouse on Central Avenue, which would bear his name. *Courtesy of Arkansas History Commission*

funeral by two farmers who sought the posted reward. Oscar Chitwood, now in custody of the deputies of the murdered sheriff, awaited trial while realizing that it was not he, but his brother, who had killed the sheriff. Oscar Chitwood would not live to go to trial—he was shot down in front of the courthouse by an angry mob while being escorted by deputies.[11]

Hot Springs would carry out its last legal hanging in June 1913, the last legal execution in Hot Springs' history. Clarence Schumann, described as "a morphine fiend," had shot his estranged wife to death. The hanging was delayed into the afternoon to allow a possible clemency from the governor, which never came. Schumann walked up

The Maurice Bath House, Hot Springs, Ark.

Maurice's first bathhouse, a wooden-frame structure opened in 1890, would be a fixture on the row for more than twenty years. By 1912, however, the superintendent of the Hot Springs reservation was becoming concerned about the state of wooden-frame bathhouses like the Maurice. Years of exposure to heat and moisture had taken a toll. With leases running out on the government land, new facilities would be required.

In their spare time at the station house this group of Hot Springs firemen practiced, with a volunteer, rescuing people from a upper-story burning building. *Courtesy of Garland County Historical Society*

This ad in the local paper drew thousands to watch "the worlds greatest birdmen" put on an aviation show at the racetrack in 1912. Put on but five years after the Wright brothers made history, the organizers of the event packed the Oaklawn stands all week with such events as "bomb dropping contests on an imaginary battleship for which the U.S. Government awards prizes."[8] Young Jimmy Ward thrilled the crowds by soaring to three thousand feet and then gliding to a landing in graceful loops.

the thirteen steps to a gallows surrounded by a high fence to block the view of the crowds, who could hear but not see the morbid procedure. Two Catholic priests came to pray with the condemned man earlier in the day and were with him when he died. His final words were "Oh, have mercy on my poor soul, dear God. Don't let there be any mistake about it. Save my soul and take me to heaven. I loved my wife. I want all to know that. I loved her better than my life. My only hope is that she is in heaven to meet me when I go."[12]

The implementation of Prohibition came in a staggered manner, as called for in the constitutional amendment, with each step bringing a new blow to the Hot Springs economy. No whiskey could be made after September 8, 1917, no beer could be brewed after May 1919, and, to allow depletion of inventory, no saloon could operate after July 1919. As the July deadline to close the saloons approached, a cloud hung over the saloon owners who would soon be, at least legally, out of business. One saloon owner went out of business with

The much-hyped young aviator Jimmie Ward was photographed in 1911 in Little Rock, a year before he flew in Hot Springs. The aviator was born Jens Wilson in 1886 to Danish immigrants in northern Minnesota. As a teenager young Jens saw no future in working in a sawmill and so left for Chicago, where by 1908 he was helping build Pullman automobiles. He developed an affinity for racing autos on the streets of Chicago, and as a result changed his name to Jimmie Ward in order to avoid losing his driver's license. Not satisfied with speed on land, Ward turned to flight and became one of the nation's best-known barnstormers in the heyday of the fad, between 1910 and 1914. According to the *Grand Forks Evening Times,* half of those who flew the fair circuit in 1911 died in accidents by the summer of 1912.[9] Ward survived but struggled after public interest passed. He invested for a time in a venture in Milwaukee building compact cars with motorcycle engines. During WWI he found his flying skills in demand and was called by the army to train fliers for combat in the skies of France. Ward died in a Florida mental hospital in 1923 at the age of thirty-seven.

a story to tell his grandchildren. John Goodine was in his saloon at 825 Central as the doomsday hour approached when he got a call from Robert Gardner, owner of a small circus. Gardner, sympathizing with Goodine's fate, offered a unique way to use up the last of his beer stock. It seemed Gardner's circus elephants had a taste for beer, and soon Goodine had two elephants bellied up to his bar, trunks swilling up beer from tubs. Tubs of more beer were taken out onto the sidewalk for other elephants to imbibe before the delighted crowds.[16]

When the bathhouses closed for the day, a lot of activity picked up in the bars and casino clubs across Central Avenue. The Indiana Club, seen in the center of the block with lights aglow, was the gambling hall where Indianapolis businessman Frank Fox was conned out of twenty thousand dollars in 1913, an action that boomeranged to cause the shutdown of gambling in Hot Springs for years to come. The wealthy man hired the William Burns Detective Agency whose pressure on local officials convinced Mayor W. W. Waters to order the gambling houses closed.[10]

Former president Theodore Roosevelt came to Hot Springs in 1910 and spoke to a packed crowd at the race track, with 1,800 school children behind him wearing red, white, and blue clothes so as to form an American flag. Flanked on the podium by Union and Confederate veterans of the Civil War, Roosevelt spoke passionately of the need for moral support for soldiers in service and the importance of conserving the nation's natural resources.

Floods and fires always brought out the photographers in Hot Springs, as during the flood of 1910 seen here. Hot Springs' unique geography in the convergence of two mountain valleys has always, even today, left the city at risk for flash floods.

Frank Head, who managed the city Opera House, opened the Princess Theater in 1910, initially putting on vaudeville acts and later silent films like *The Inside of the White Slave Traffic,* as seen in the *Sentinel Record* newspaper ad. In 1914 there were actually movies being made in Hot Springs. The film *Human Shield* was so named because of an escaping convict using an office stenographer as a shield from police bullets. Locations included the Army and Navy Hospital with a finale fight to the death in the Ouachita River.

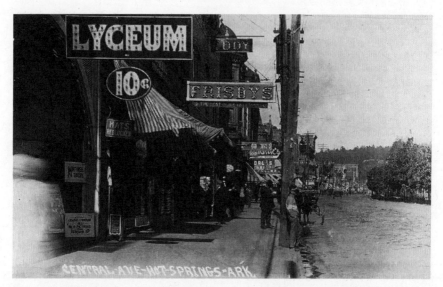

Among the oldest theaters in Hot Springs was the Lyceum, seen here in 1910 when admission was ten cents. Ads in the *Sentinel Record* sought to draw audiences to see *Dante's Inferno* with a "go to hell" enticement.

Samuel Fordyce owned the stately Victorian Palace Bathhouse for some two decades, but competition for the upscale bather led him to tear it down and erect the Fordyce Bathhouse on the site. The most expensive of all the Bathhouse Row's facilities, the Spanish Rennaissance-style building was touted by Mr. Fordyce as having "walls of veined Italian marble rising from mosaiced tiles, stately staircases of pink marble . . . that make a great lounging court reminiscent of the luxury of old Rome."[17]

The Fordyce Bath House, Hot Springs, Arkansas.

OCCUPIES SITE OF OLD PALACE BATH HOUSE.
JNO. F. MANIER, MGR.

By today's standards not even a highway, the gravel road that finally linked Hot Springs with Little Rock in 1915 was the cause of great celebration by civic leaders who hoped it would bring more visitors to the resort town. As a part of the dedication a motorcade left Little Rock at 7:00 AM and arrived in Hot Springs at 11:30, completing the fifty-mile trip in only four and a half hours. *Courtesy of Garland County Historical Society*

CORNOR STONE LAYING
ROANOKE BAPTIST CHURCH
J. K. HENDERSON. PASTOR
AUG. 8. 1915. HOT SPRINGS. ARK

The black community of Hot Springs dedicated a community anchor in 1915 that remains steadfast to this day: the Roanoke Baptist Church. The church was originally organized in 1868 by former slaves, one of whom had come from Roanoke, Virginia—hence the name. The church still serves its congregation in modern day Hot Springs. *Courtesy of Garland County Historical Society*

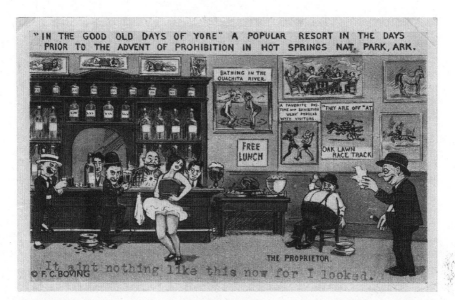

"IN THE GOOD OLD DAYS OF YORE" A POPULAR RESORT IN THE DAYS PRIOR TO THE ADVENT OF PROHIBITION IN HOT SPRINGS NAT. PARK, ARK.

Prohibition was a law many in Hot Springs opposed. Some flagrantly flouted it while others profited by making jokes on postcards.

The coming of a new road would give Hot Springs residents reason to start shopping for automobiles. The Market Street Garage opened in 1908 to serve the new horseless carriages, staying open twenty-four hours a day. In 1915 Hot Springs counted 245 automobiles, but by 1925 the count would rise to more than 4,000.

The COMO Hotel, seen on the left in profile by the streetlights of the city, opened in 1915 at the junction of Central, Ouachita, Market and Olive Streets, hence the name of the hotel. In a rare nighttime photograph, the illuminated streetcar is heading north on Central passing the Garrison Hotel on the right. The COMO was the dream of Edward Hoadley Johnson, who wrapped it in a unique shiny white Tiffany brick created by the famed New York jeweler.

The city sent a number of its young men off to the military in World War I. Company C, posed before a local church, were mustered into active duty in August 1917 as the war against the Germans raged in France. The Hot Springs Selective Service Board declared nonessential occupations to be "pool hall operators, cigar clerks, fountain dispensers, cigar makers, porters, ushers and movie ticket takers, and hotel clerks,"[19] making all holding such jobs subject to being drafted. *Courtesy of Garland County Historical Society*

World War I brought frenetic activity to Hot Springs along with many patients returning from the battlefield for care at the town's Army and Navy Hospital. In this photograph circa 1917 a growing number of automobiles compete for room on Central in front of Schneck's drugstore and Kress's dime store. During the Depression soda-fountain clerks at Schneck's earned forty cents an hour, about what a well-dressed bank teller down the street would have made. They worked out a deal with ticket takers at the Paramount Theater to swap lunches at the fountain counter in exchange for free admission to the movies.[18] The Schneck building remains today as a part of the historic district.

Thousands of army troops were trained at Camp Pike outside of Little Rock, and they often came to Hot Springs on their leave days. One soldier posed atop one of the big birds at the Ostrich Farm, a bag over the bird's head so as not to panic it. Commanders at Camp Pike found the soldiers were coming to the spa city for more than the ostriches and asked Hot Springs city hall for an "arbitrary order that unless the houses of immorality of the city were closed, the government would issue some sort of edict against soldiers spending their weekends there."[20] The city fathers' response was not to close the brothels but to candidly tell the operators to take a lower profile.

The Howard, Furnished Rooms, 510 Central Avenue, opposite Bath House Row and U. S. Reservation. Hot Springs, Ark. S. Bowman, Prop.

It seemed gambling, both on large and small scales, was everywhere in Hot Springs. The unique, and budget, Howard Hotel on Central Avenue was the site of a violent death for card player James Ray after he was accused of running a crooked game in one of the hotel's rooms. Two armed men crashed the game—taking two thousand dollars from the gathered players—and fled. A week later when the game resumed, Ray evicted a man accused of cheating. The man soon returned with gun in hand, fatally shot Ray, and wounded a second man before fleeing. Dozens of panicked gamblers rushed out on the man's heels, trying to get out of the second floor of the small hotel.

CHAPTER EIGHT

The Spa City's Roaring Twenties
1920–1930

The 1920s would see in Hot Springs the prosperity enjoyed by the nation as a whole during this period, but it was mitigated by adverse attention for not only natural and man-made disaster but also the return of wide-open gambling and, in the minds of some, the related crime and vice. In the midst of all this, however, Congress would designate in 1921 what had been a federal reservation as a national park, the Hot Springs National Park. It would be a decade of contrasts, of vices ranging from illicit gambling and brothels to the flaunting of Prohibition, and of the severity of the Great Depression.

The colorful politician Leo McLaughlin would start a twenty-year run as the resort town's mayor and would, in his own interest and the professed interest of business, throw the town wide open for gambling and regulated prostitution. Few people in the town's history, for better or worse, would have more of an impact on the city.

Along with gambling, prostitution would be a hotly debated topic. Dr. Oliver Wenger, in his federally appointed duty of fighting venereal disease, had stepped into the role in 1919 and was working hard in Hot Springs by 1922 when the spa became a center of federal research into the disease. Dr. Wenger fingered prostitution as the root cause of the problem. The U.S. Public Health Service for whom he worked was taking aim at the "evils of the unregulated commercial dance halls." The claim was that sexual immorality took root in such places and posed a threat to young people, since the dance halls were "frequently connected with saloons and so-called hotels which encourage immoral behavior." The Interdepartmental Social Hygiene Board hired a woman to survey seven Hot Springs dance halls in order to confirm the theory. In her report the investigator wrote that while she observed

Death rode the rails just outside Hot Springs on a cold February day in 1921 when a train jackknifed off the tracks. Engineer Jack Sullivan, age thirty-six, and train fireman Felix Blackburn, age thirty, were killed when a rotten cross tie collapsed under the weight of the train, causing it to overturn and toss the baggage car over the engine.[1]
Courtesy of Garland County Historical Society

"Diamond House is the Victim of Big Robbery," read the newspaper headline. Jaccard's Jewlery, which occupied part of the lower level of the Hotel Pullman, fell victim to the slight-of-hand theft of $17,000 in diamonds in 1921. "Timing his work to perfection some smart sneak thief yesterday afternoon lifted a tray of fine diamond rings from the show window of the Jaccard branch of this city."[2]

The Texas Oil Company, forerunner of TEXACO, opened this Roman-styled service station on the north end of Central in 1921, helping fund the town's library by leasing land owned by the library association. The station building was a landmark for many years before being removed; the spot is a parking lot today.

no profanity she did take note of "men of cheap, sporty type, some of whom were accompanied by girls similar in appearance." She found "couples engaged in improper dancing" and noted several girls in one location that she deemed "were of the prostitute type."[4]

While violence was a part of the moonshine trade, resulting in death at times for both law enforcement and violators alike, a softer story appeared in the *Sentinel Record* on September 11, 1926. "AGED MOONSHINER COMPLETES FINAL SENTENCES TODAY IN COUNTY BASTILE . . . After Over Half a Century Passed in Manufacturing and Selling Illicit Whiskey, Elisha Fate Robertson Comes to Conclusion

Maurice Connelly, a nephew of the county judge, was fatally shot when he came home and surprised a burglar in 1922. The accused was a paroled felon, "Punk" Harris, who was arrested and jailed. A mob broke the man out of his cell and lynched him in the square. The *Sentinel Record* said of the hanging, "The lynching in this city yesterday morning of the negro Harris will put an end to the house robberies that have been prevalent for some time. Aside from avenging the murder of Maurice Connelly, the lynching will put the fear into the criminal class which invades the homes of people."[3] *Courtesy of Garland County Historical Society*

Product Entails Only Trouble for All Who Handle It—Says He is Through and Officers Who Know Him Put Full Faith in Old Man's Statement." "Uncle Fate," at the age of 72, stated he had been making "likker" since he was eighteen years old. He had been in and out of jails and Tucker Prison for years. "Before they passed this prohibition law, I could get by easier than now, but even then my money went, just the same, but since the dry law passed it's been a heap harder to get by."[9]

A lot of things would be harder in Hot Springs before the tumultuous decade of the 1920s came to a close.

When smoke started curling through the floor of the Arlington Hotel in 1923, the fire was at first thought containable, but soon ambulances were lining up out of concern that such faith was misplaced. Among the evacuated guests were Mrs. Joe T. Robinson, wife of the Arkansan U.S. senator, and famed detective William Pinkerton. The detective had been sitting on the porch smoking a cigar, believing it was only a minor fire in the kitchen, until the flames prevented him from returning to his room to retrieve his belongings.

The April 1923 fire, caused apparently by faulty wiring, engulfed the thirty-three-year-old hotel. Rescue accounts in the next days paper wrote, "Several women, some quite elderly, had never been on a ladder before, one slightly crippled, came down three flights."[5] Soldiers from the Army and Navy Hospital came on the scene with gas masks and raced down smoke-clogged hallways trying to make sure all were rescued.

The morning of April 5 revealed the death of a fireman, a father of seven, and only a few brick walls standing of the grand Arlington that had once stretched along Central Avenue. The *Sentinel Record* gave credit for the survival of all the guests to many of the hotel's black employees: "Many of the guests of the Arlington Hotel have asked to say a word for the splendid work of the colored help of the hotel during the fire. They proved themselves brave, saved valuable property through stifling smoke, bellboys, porters, hallmen, waiters, elevator operators, were on the job. We were guests of the Arlington, their Arlington."[6]

A few weeks after fire destroyed the Arlington Hotel, a record flood swept an estimated four-to-nine feet of debris-filled water through the downtown business district, tossing automobiles around like toys. "Upon its crest here and there were human forms, unfortunates who had been too late in striking for safety. Hundreds of automobiles slipped and grated and then finally shot the waves, and were carried through the valley. Many of them had occupants, frantic screaming women, and little children, panic stricken and crazed by an experience that caused them to face death."[7] The only recorded fatality was Bertha Christianson, wife of the chef at the Army and Navy. She died when her hair became entangled in the steering wheel of her flood-borne car. After the floodwaters drained away much of the pavement of Central Avenue was found to have been peeled away.

Before the end of 1924 a new Arlington Hotel opened across Fountain Street from the one burned the year before. At a cost of some $2 million Samuel Fordyce and investors pushed construction with shifts often around the clock, paying bricklayers $1.50 an hour and carpenters $1 an hour. The 1924 hotel still anchors the north end of Bathhouse Row today.

The five-hundred-room hotel included the resort town's first radio station, with a broad-cast booth, a desk, and accompaniment from the piano on the right. The five-hundred-watt transmitter sat atop the hotel; the broadcast studio was a converted hotel room. The assigned station letters, *KTHS,* were said to stand for "Kum to Hot Springs."[8] Reaching into parts of twenty-three states, the station helped launch the careers of Chester Lauck and Norris Goff of Mena as "Lum & Abner." *Courtesy of Garland County Historical Society*

The faculty of the National Baseball School for Youngsters visited the new Arlington Hotel in 1924. Per the back of the photo, sixty-five boys from sixteen different states enrolled. Left to right: Leslie Mann, former major-league star and national director of the Amateur Baseball Association; Rogers Hornsby, of the St. Louis Cardinals; Ray Doan, director of the school; and Jack Ryan, the Cardinals' coach.

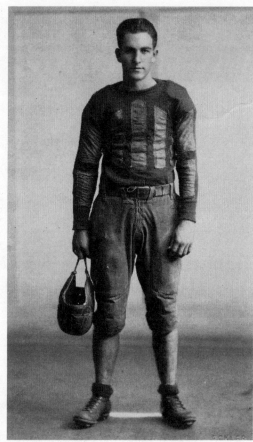

Few athletes excelled at so many sports as did Hot Springs High's Paul Markle in the 1920s. The movie-star-handsome young man is seen in his boxing togs, his football uniform, at top left with the 1927 AAA district-champion basketball team, and at center bottom with the Rotary-sponsored baseball team.

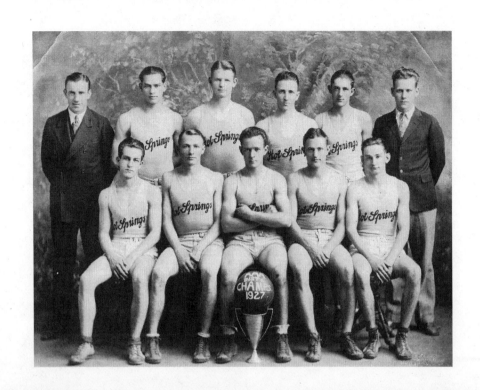

above: Prohibition led to a booming moonshine industry in the hills surrounding Hot Springs. Sheriff Jim Floyd, in front holding a shotgun, occasionally raided stills. Municipal judge Verne Ledgerwood had little heart for enforcing the law against liquor, however, commenting that "the prohibition law has not been a success. In my opinion it never will be. Public sentiment makes or breaks any law, and public sentiment is against bone-dry prohibition."[10] *Courtesy of Garland County Historical Society*

right: Liquor was illegal in the 1920s, but moonshine jugs and a log bar were favorite props at the Happy Hollow photograph gallery.

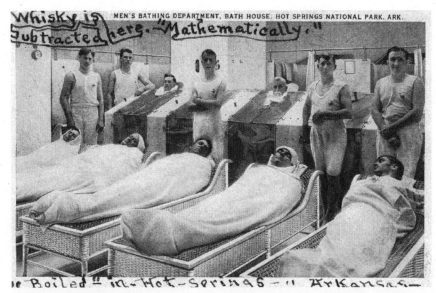

MEN'S BATHING DEPARTMENT, BATH HOUSE, HOT SPRINGS NATIONAL PARK, ARK.

Whisky is subtracted here. "Mathematically."

ie Boiled" in Hot Springs "Arkansas

One bather around 1925 suggested that the steamy bathhouse was where "whiskey is subtracted . . . mathematically."

Hot Springs National Park ranger James Cary, dressed like this unidentified man and driving a similar government-issued coupe, was murdered while on duty in 1927. Ranger Cary had been hired in 1923 at an annual salary of a thousand dollars. A lack of trust on the part of FBI director J. Edgar Hoover led to the assignment of a special agent to investigate the murder, but nobody was ever convicted. Ranger Cary was buried beneath a marker that read, "Faithful to his trust, even unto death." *Courtesy of Garland County Historical Society*

Alcohol, including the making and consumption of beer, was illegal in 1926, and yet here a train pulls in beside a building bearing the sign for the Anheuser Busch Brewing Association. The tower of the Eastman Hotel looms in the background.

above and on opposite page: St. Joseph's hospital opened its new facility on Whittington Avenue in 1927 with 157 beds to serve the bustling resort city. This five-story building replaced the sixty-bed wooden-frame building that the Sisters of Mercy had operated for may years. St. Joseph's nursing staff included many nuns who carried out their duties wearing white habits. Caring for newborns in the nursery or taking an X-ray of a patient's foot was all in a day's work. *Courtesy of Garland County Historical Society*

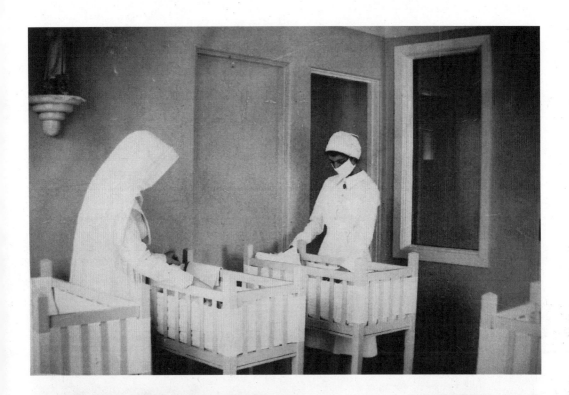

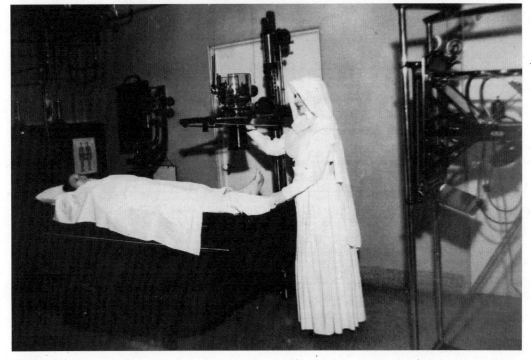

Dugan-Stuart Medical Bldg. Southern Grill W. S. JACOBS, Prop. Waukesha Hotel J. A. CAMERON, Prop.

above: William "W. S." Jacobs, while regulating all the gambling in the city, also owned his own gambling halls like the Southern Grill seen in the center of this post-card circa 1928. Other gambling places soon opened with Jacob's approval and franchise fees labeled "fines" paid to the city coffers. The Southern Grill, located across the street from the Arlington, was among the most visible of the town's gambling parlors.

right: A frequent patron at the Belvedere and other Hot Springs nightspots was "Bottles" Capone, brother of Chicago gangster Al Capone. The better known of the Capone brothers, Al was partial to the Arlington Hotel, reportedly even renting the entire fourth floor on occasion for his entourage.
Courtesy of Garland County Historical Society

W. S. Jacobs combined promotions for both his Hot Springs gambling clubs, the Southern Grill downtown and the Belvedere out on the Little Rock highway. The business drew the ire of antigambling interests, especially in 1928 when a drunken school teacher was reported dancing nude atop a dining table. Both the gambling and the alcohol were against the law.

Hot Springs' wide-open lifestyle and nightlife drew famous figures of the day, like boxing champion Jack Dempsey, on the left, dining with his wife and actor Rudolph Valentino at the Arlington Hotel. *Courtesy of Garland County Historical Society*

McClard's BBQ, perhaps the best-known name in Hot Springs dining, got its start in this rustic tourist camp in 1928. Alex and Gladys McClard operated a group of small cabins called Westside Tourist Camp. One guest, after staying two months, lacked the money to pay his bill but told the McClard's, "I'll tell you what I have got: I've got the best recipe for barbecue sauce and I'll give it to you."[11] The crumpled-up paper led to changing the business's name to Westside Bar-B-Que, and decades later the eating establishment remains among the best known in the state. *Courtesy of Garland County Historical Society*

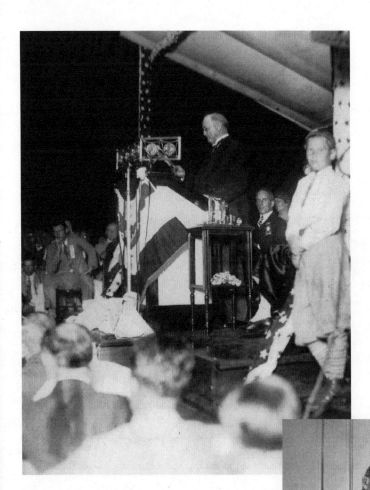

Arkansas's Senator Joe T. Robinson came to Hot Springs to formally accept the Democratic Party's nomination to run as the candidate for the vice presidency of the United States. His speech to some 25,000 of his fellow Arkansans was the greatest political event in the history of the state up to that time and was broadcast across the nation on radio station KTHS. Robinson and New York governor Al Smith, who headed the Democratic ticket, lost to Hubert Hoover in the 1928 election. *Courtesy of Garland County Historical Society*

Hot Springs National Park, Arkansas

At a cost of $2.5 million Hot Springs saw a new Army and Navy Hospital rise on the site of the one that had been built to care for aging Civil War veterans in the preceding century. The hospital was closed in the 1960s, and the building was given to the state for conversion to a rehabilitation center.

CHAPTER NINE

Depression, an Expanding Federal Presence, and Slow Recovery
1930–1940

As the 1930s opened the National Park Service began to flex its muscle, bringing in landscape architect Thomas Vint and architect Charles Peterson. To meet their charge to improve the park the two men laid out the design for the broad promenade that to the present day fronts Bathhouse Row. Over the objections of the bathhouse owners the two men pushed through a system of central collection and distribution of the thermal waters to all the bathhouses and hotels.

A few steps removed from government-controlled Bathhouse Row, Hot Springs garnered continual attention for its reputation for sin and vice often interlaced with stories about the town's colorful mayor, Leo McLaughlin.

Hot Springs got widely read national publicity in August 1931 that it would have preferred to avoid when *Collier's* magazine published an eight-page spread entitled "Sin takes a Hot Bath." The reporter took a number of witty jabs at the city, at Mayor McLaughlin, and at gambling czar W. S. Jacobs. "The name of this one-man government is Leo P. McLaughlin. . . . His philosophy is 'Make the visitor pay but give him so much fun that he forgets the price.'"

"Gangsters and clergymen, racketeers and dear old ladies with rusty joints, bankers and two-bit chislers, kings and communists, gunmen and vegetarians, journalists and respectables—all, all are welcome to Hot Springs to cure their aches, indulge their weaknesses, cultivate their virtues." The article detailed the out-of-control gambling operations and the scandals that had beset Hot Springs early in the century and how McLaughlin's machine had anointed Jacobs to regulate gambling in the city. "So Mr. Jacobs was chosen. He is a large,

Hot Springs celebrated its hundredth anniversary as a federal reservation in 1932 with a week-long celebration capped by a mile-long parade. One parade float approaching the Arlington Hotel was a Southern "mammy." *Courtesy of Garland County Historical Society*

dark, taciturn man who, legend has it, hasn't exhibited an emotion since the moment of his birth, when it is further alleged, he uttered the battle cry of freedom." The reporter noted that "gambling was as much a part of the life of Hot Springs as steel is of Pittsburgh's, as beef of Chicago's, as textiles of Philadelphia's, as movies of Hollywood's. Stop gambling and the baths could be used to wash flivvers in. Let the baths fail and—well, you might as well give the valley back to the Indians. Such, anyway, were the arguments."

The *Collier's* article also explained to the readers the division of Hot Springs, with the federally-owned Bathhouse Row on one side of Central Avenue, where there was no vice, and the other side of the street, lined by the hotels and gambling halls regulated by W. S. Jacobs. The system of fines paid by the gamblers was explained in a way not likely ever in print before.

> The fines assessed against the gamblers is not an arbitrary one; it depends upon the city's budget—how much the city is going to need, how much it owes. For example, there is a sewage-disposal plant that the city is about to build—a four-hundred-thousand-dollar project designed to safeguard to the health of the little valley hamlet which must take care of 250,000 visitors each year.

above and opposite top: Parade watchers lined Central Avenue in front of the Fordyce Bathhouse, catching a close look at bicycles from decades past. The winner among the twenty-nine floats entered in the parade was described in the *Sentinel Record:* "Its setting was the front stoop of a pioneer home of the South. In the foreground a little pickaninny was lying in the grass, basking in the sun on his stomach, and ready to be called on any errand. An old Negro mammy sat in a rocker on the lawn caring for a little white baby. An old butler posed as if to serve a mistress who stood on the portico with an older child at her side."[1] The float had been entered by the local chapter of the Daughters of the Confederacy. *Courtesy of Garland County Historical Society*

Singer Kate Smith came to town in 1934, posing at one of the Hot Springs but choosing to stay at the Mountain Valley Hotel twelve miles north of the city. It was not the best of choices, for while she watched from the lawn, the twenty-six-room hotel, with her luggage inside, burned to the ground. She finished her vacation at the Arlington. *Courtesy of Garland County Historical Society*

Mountain Valley Hotel, 12 Miles North of Hot Springs, Ark., Fine Drive.

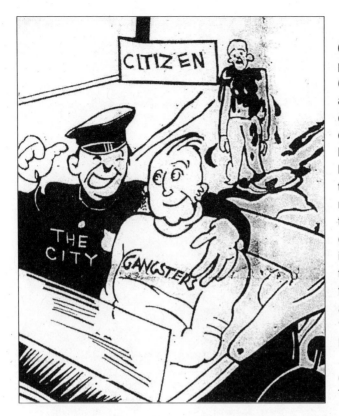

One local newspaper, the *Public Opinion*, published an editorial cartoon critical of city leaders, especially of Mayor Leo McLaughlin, over their seeming coziness with out-of-town gangsters and expressed its views in an editorial cartoon. A headline in the paper in 1933 asked questions, "Why do Gangsters Like Hot Springs? . . . Is it the Climate or the Protection They Get?"[2]

Were it to meet the requirements of the permanent population—16,000 souls, the huge majority of whom work either for the baths, for the hotels or for Mr. Jacobs—a hundred-thousand dollar plant, or none, would do. If it weren't for the baths and Mr. Jacobs no plant at all would do nicely because there would be no Hot Springs. How, then, do you suppose this small wage-earning town would build a four-hundred-thousand-dollar sanitary outfit? By imposing ruinous excises upon the hotels? By taxing its non-industrial citizenry? Not at all! No. Mr. Jacobs and his house managers will take care of it. Those periodic fines will build the sewage-disposal plant that the United States Health Service and the health authorities of Arkansas demand. Thank you, Mr. Jacobs, call again. . . . Similarly, who is going to provide the money for street paving and cleaning? Gambling produces it. Mr. Jacobs and his associates have contributed as much as $40,000 a year to Hot Springs streets.

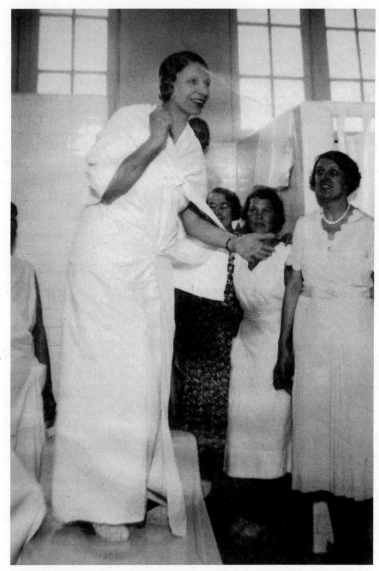

Famed evangelist Aimee Semple McPherson came to Hot Springs in the early 1930s for a bath but could not resist preaching a sermon, even while dressed in a bathrobe. *Courtesy of Garland County Historical Society*

The Hot Springs gambling halls had been shuttered for a decade when Leo McLaughlin was elected mayor in 1927 with the support of those intent on reopening the casinos. The new mayor soon tapped William Jacobs, seen here, to control the reopening gaming houses. Jacobs had been active in Hot Springs gambling prior to 1913 and was considered an honest gambling kingpin whom the mayor could expect to make sure the city got its share of the proceeds.

The *Collier's* article made a lot of the fact that Hot Springs had little in the way of serious crime.

> Stick-ups are virtually nonexistent in Hot Springs. The enjoyable truth is that Hot Springs, where you can do practically anything you can pay for, which lacks practically all the common civic prohibitions, which recognizes none of the conventional prohibitions and asks only that the visitor observe the right of his neighbor to enjoy himself in his own peculiar way, has no crime waves and very few crimes. . . . Now and then they have a murder, but you have to go back several years to find one that involved a visitor or had its inception in gambling. Now and then a hillbilly, over stimulated by the corn whiskey of his own Ozarks, will shoot his neighbor over some passionate difference such as ownership of a still, a hog, a brook, a customer or a woman; or a Negro will decide that another Negro has lived long enough. But these

unhappy incidents are infrequent. . . . Not that ordinary morals have anything to do with it. Crime is bad for business and Mr. McLaughlin is a thoroughly businesslike gentleman.[3]

Hot Springs would also in the 1930s draw notice as a haven for gangsters taking time off from their distant criminal empires for some R&R, and also perhaps for some lesser hoods actually practicing their trade in the city. Unlike most of the local media, the weekly *Public Opinion* newspaper was often a harsh critic of Mayor McLaughlin's political machine; the paper alleged that city officials, especially the police, were too cozy with the criminals inhabiting Hot Springs and were not looking out for the security of law-abiding citizens. One headline on September 29, 1933, asked the question, "Why do Gangsters Like Hot Springs?. . . . Is it the Climate or the Protection They Get?" The paper went after small-time criminals as well as gangsters, frequently attacking the resurgence of "drummers," paid solicitors working surreptitiously for local tourist businesses. It was alleged that Mayor McLaughlin allowed the practice to creep back into the city after it had been largely shut down a decade before by the Interior Department. "Respectable visitors, taxi drivers, and the managers and owners of all rated hotels and rooming houses object to the coercion applied by the rabble of cheap rooming house drummers who pester incoming passengers at the railroad and bus stations and carry some of them to destinations free of charge in motor cars operating without taxi licenses." City officials had been dismissing such concerns by saying that Hot Springs was "just one big family" and everyone ought to work together. Said the *Public Opinion* of such a defense, "If you are in right and an abiding member of 'just one big family,' you may get by with one license plate for two cars. It has been done."[4] The town's reputation for sheltering mobsters was further solidified with the visits of Al Capone and his brother "Bottles" Capone and the high profile arrests of Charles "Lucky" Luciano and Alvin "Creepy" Karpis. J. Edgar Hoover, the FBI boss, was especially furious at local Hot Springs law enforcement for coddling Karpis. The town's gambling interest would pay a larger price for the ire of Arkansas governor Carl Bailey over the harboring of Luciano. In 1937 he dispatched a caravan of state police to raid and shut down the gambling clubs. The gaming tables and roulette wheels were later burned in a bonfire in front of the state capitol in Little Rock. An appeal by the Hot Springs business community to the governor that

Pres. Franklin D. Roosevelt came to visit in 1936, marking the hundredth birthday of the state. Senator Joe T. Robison and Mayor Leo McLaughlin posed aboard his train as the president disembarked before huge crowds. His legs crippled by polio a decade before, Roosevelt was aided off the train by his secret service agents.

As was FDR's trademark, he traveled from the train station to the Arlington Hotel in an open-topped car, shaking hands along the route. Before touring the Fordyce Bathhouse, FDR gave a speech praising the state: "For me this has been a glorious day. While I have been to Arkansas before this, my visits have been too much like a bird of passage and this is the first chance I've had to see the state at closer range. . . . I have seen your parks, I have seen the beauty of your mountains and rivers. Arkansas can claim every warrant for the name 'Wonder State.'"[5]

While President Roosevelt was elsewhere, his wife, Eleanor, was dining with Arkansas's first lady and U.S. senator Hattie Carraway. One *Sentinel Record* headline proclaimed "Hill Dwellers Are Among Thousands Here to See FDR." The story profiled one "rugged mountaineer" who arrived a day early to see the president, having ridden a mule thirty miles to reach the city.[6] *Courtesy of Garland County Historical Society*

their tourist trade needed the "controlled" gambling would soon cause Bailey to relent and allow the resumption of gambling, continuing a chapter in the city's history that would not conclude for decades to come.

Hot Springs did get a ray of economic sunshine when, under the leadership of Mayor Leo McLaughlin, Oaklawn Park race track reopened after being closed down for fifteen years. Technically the opening was illegal, but fifteen thousand people packed the stands. It was enough to convince Governor Marion Futrell to sign the bill legalizing gambling on the horses, overriding objections like those from a Benton legislator who proclaimed, "Every dollar of revenue you say this bill will bring in, smells of the brimstone of Hades."[7]

In 1938 Hot Springs streets, packed with automobiles, saw the demise of the streetcars in favor of buses. The streetcars and their tracks had taken up space deemed necessary for automobiles and their parking spaces. *Courtesy of Garland County Historical Society*

CHAPTER TEN

Political and World Conflicts
Impact the Spa City
1940–1950

The decade of the 1940s opened with a census report of Hot Springs' population at 31,054. The forties would be among the most memorable decades in the history of the city. The self-serving maneuvering of Mayor Leo McLauglin would continue, but his luck would run out before the decade's end.

In the midst of all the press and political maneuvering over gambling, Hot Springs in 1941 made a little-noted entry into the history books' chapter on civil rights. A black congressman from Illinois, Arthur W. Mitchell, was denied Pullman-car accommodations by the Rock Island Railroad while en route to Hot Springs for a visit. In hearing *Mitchell v. United States* the Supreme Court, noting such accommodations were readily available to whites, found that the discrimination against Congressman Mitchell was a violation of the Interstate Commerce Act.[1]

The opponents of gambling, with hopes of what new governor Homer Adkins might do, were able to get a grand jury impaneled to examine the evidence. One of the witnesses turned out to be Mayor Leo McLauglin, who reported that for a three-month period in the spring of 1941 a total of $250,365 in gambling fines were collected by the city, enough to run the city's street department.[2] Still, the final power to act rested in Little Rock with Governor Atkins, who had pledged to enforce the law against gambling. Under threat of a raid by the state police, many of the gambling halls and bookmakers closed up shop on their own. When the governor failed to act immediately, the club owners' complacency, tempered with hope, set in, and soon the town was gambling again, although lookouts were posted on the

The four-hundredth anniversary in 1941 of the legendary visit to the hot springs by Hernando de Soto gave Hot Springs a reason to hold a two-week pageant it called "Saga of Waters," complete with performers in Native American garb. *Courtesy of Garland County Historical Society*

Little Rock highway outside of Hot Springs to give early warning if the state police were sighted approaching the city.

Another World War Touches Hot Springs

Amid the uncertainty as to when or if the authorities in Little Rock would move against the Hot Springs gambling industry, events on the world stage overtook the local headlines. The Japanese attacked Pearl Harbor on December 7, 1941, and in the coming weeks and months many of the town's doctors and bathhouse employees would either enlist or be drafted into the armed forces. Even the supplies needed to run the bathhouses, like bath mitts and thermometers, came into short supply as materials were diverted to the manufacture of war materiel.

As war raged around the globe, the next chapter in Hot Springs' decades-long love affair with gambling would open in January 1942 when the state police unexpectedly arrived in force, apparently from the direction of Malvern and thereby circumventing the lookouts posted on the Little Rock highway. As they descended on the gambling halls, "telephones were torn loose from the walls, loud-speaking equipment was dismantled, wall charts, form books and similar accessories were loaded into the rear of state police cars, and roulette wheels and dice tables were destroyed on the spot."[3]

Was Homer Adkins finally a governor of Arkansas who intended to keep the vow his predecessors had made but defaulted upon, to shut down Hot Springs' gambling? The gambling industry kept hoping it was not so, that the governor would tire of the raids and divert his attention to other matters. However, through much of 1942 the gamblers would try to reopen, mostly as lower-profile horse-book parlors, and the state police would sweep through with warrants and finally even arrest some of the operators. Offenders were usually longtime Hot Springs residents and tended to get off lightly, as local officials treated the offenses as misdemeanors with no contradiction from the Garland County prosecuting attorney, much to the irritation of the officials in Little Rock. Three and half years into the stalemate, the governor's attention did indeed gradually shift to other concerns, most especially his unsuccessful race for the U.S. Senate against J. William Fulbright.

"HOT SPRINGS, ARK. FROM MOUNTAIN DRIVE"   5-14

With the Army and Navy Hospital bursting at the seams with returning soldiers from WWII, the military purchased the massive Eastman Hotel, seen to the right in this photograph, for $550,000. It was joined to the hospital by a sky bridge, making an annex to care for hundreds of additional patients returned from the battlefield.

Wives and girlfriends often joined soldiers on R&R in Hot Springs and were the subject of countless photographs, like the one of this unidentified couple atop Hot Springs Mountain.

During the war the uniforms of the military and of the National Park Service rangers mixed along Bathhouse Row, as did the habits of the nuns and uniforms of the Women's Army Corps at St. Joseph's Hospital. *Courtesy of Garland County Historical Society*

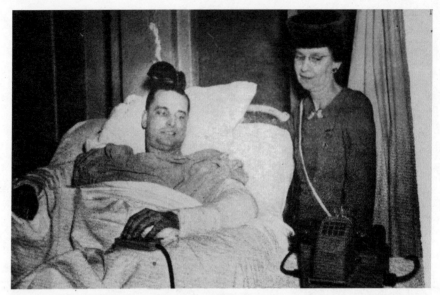

Wounded soldiers back from WWII got some help from those devoted to veterans of another war. At the Army and Navy Hospital, Miss Ruth Hardin, president of the Arkansas division of the United Daughters of the Confederacy, presented a book projector to a soldier who could not use his arms.

Hot Springs as Military Redistribution Center

In August 1944 the military took control of all the major hotels in the city, including the Majestic, the DeSoto, and the Park, in order to provide lodging for military men. Soldiers with wives were given rooms at the Arlington. The military had surveyed some twenty cities around the nation and selected Hot Springs to be the redistribution center for returning troops from the west-central states. The returning soldiers were given a twenty-one-day furlough before reporting to the Hot Springs Redistribution Center, where for the next fourteen days their military records would be updated and they would get any needed physical or dental treatment. The plan was for some 2,500 servicemen and women each month to be rotated through the program, and the Hot Springs economy would benefit greatly. A "Redistribution Station" guidebook was given to the arriving stream of returning servicemen, with a foreword by Maj. Gen. Richard Donovan, commander of the operation in Hot Springs. "This Redistribution Station has been estab-

During WWII a COMO guest took his camera to the rooftop of the hotel at the prominent intersection. With the lens pointed back up Central Avenue the result was a commanding view of the distant Arlington Hotel, the Army and Navy Hospital to the right, and next to it the venerable Eastman Hotel, which was taken over by the army during the war as a hospital annex.

lished to study your physical condition and your qualifications so that you can be assigned where you will be most useful to the Army." Perhaps mindful of the vice and temptations available within sight of the Army and Navy Hospital, General Donavon went on to say, "You are reminded that as soldiers you will be expected to conduct yourselves as gentlemen. As overseas veterans, your appearance and your conduct will be under close scrutiny, and the impressions you create on others

Despite the war raging Mayor McLaughlin found time to visit his box at Oaklawn. His companion was focused on the horses coming around the turn, but the mayor was fixed on the photographer. McLaughlin, along with the local business community, had pushed a bill through the legislature in 1935 making legal horse racing and wagering. *Courtesy of Garland County Historical Society*

will be strong and lasting ones. . . . Have a good time, enjoy your liberties, meet your schedules and be considerate of the comfort and convenience of others."[4]

An event a few months after the war ended clearly demonstrated once more Mayor Leo McLaughlin's lack of judgment. The local officers' club at the Army and Navy Hospital put in a few slot machines with the goal of providing recreation for the patients and raising a little money for the club. How, the officers questioned, could anyone seriously object, given the obvious gambling going on in the city? But Uncle Sam's boys obviously had not met the mayor and his brother George. Word got back to George McLaughlin about the five slot machines at the officers' club, and he immediately protested to his brother the mayor that these brought unfair competition with the slot machines he had operating around the city. McLaughlin promptly dispatched the police to confiscate the soldiers' machines, reminding them that "the slots were illegal"; the five machines were destroyed at the county jail. A protest by the commanding officer at the hospital

Tap-dancer "Bojangles" visited Hot Springs, tap dancing his way across town to the delight of the packed wartime city. The entertainer, known as the "King of Tapology," tap danced from the Phillips Drive-In on Park Avenue to the Pythian Bathhouse on Malvern Avenue. *Courtesy of Garland County Historical Society*

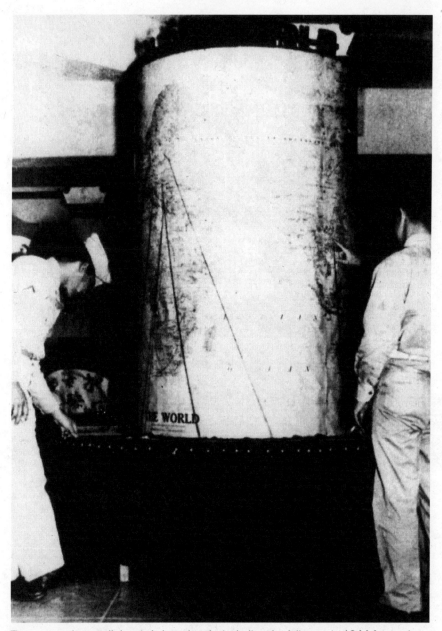

The army took over all the city's large hotels, including the Arlington in 1944 for use by returning troops being processed through the designated redistribution center. The soldiers seen here were tracking the progress of the war on a map in the lobby of the hotel. At the close of the war all the hotels, except the Eastman, were returned to their owners.

Soldiers were drawn to the attractive clerks in the shop of the Arlington Hotel, a world apart from the battlefields from which many of the men had returned only weeks before. Taken over by the military, the hotel's thousand-seat auditorium was converted to a movie theater for soldiers for whom room, meals, and entertainment were free. Visiting spouses were accommodated at a charge of twenty-five dollars for a ten-day stay.

sparked a further rebuke from city hall in the form of a new policy: the military police assigned to Hot Springs could no longer have an office at the city's police station, nor could they any longer ride in city police cars.[6]

 With an ugly election campaign underway in which returning servicemen led by Sid McMath sought to challenge the McLaughlin machine, a new, widely read exposé of Hot Springs appeared in the July 1946 issue of the national *Saturday Evening Post* magazine, entitled "THE TOWN WITHOUT A LID." The reporter wandered about town, doing interviews and making his own observations. "Hot Springs was deposited by its innocent founders in Western Arkansas, where to the relief of the rest of Arkansas, it has remained, oblivious of the curious ways of the outside, law-abiding world. It has grown into a city that steadfastly refuses to relax and behave as nice little cities should. . . . Most of the things are against the law in Hot Springs, but this is simply

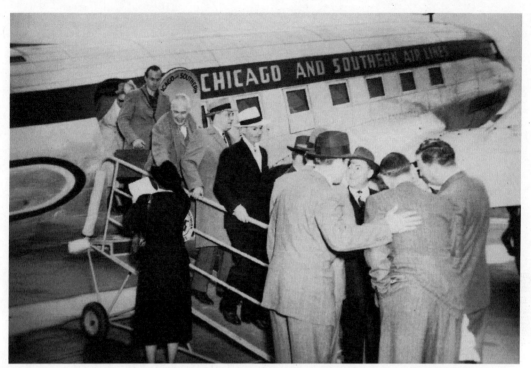

After WWII, amid controversy the city council briefly named the new Hot Springs airport for Mayor Leo McLaughlin, as inscribed for a time in the marble of the passenger lobby in the terminal. During the war years McLaughlin had to fend off a federal grand-jury probe concerning the 1943 elections at which all the poll workers were reputed to be gamblers, judges, and clerks aligned with the mayor. Despite the fact that 735 ballots were thrown out, the mayor remained in office. The Chicago & Southwestern Air Line made use of the new airfield. Seen here is a group of arriving businessmen disembarking around 1947. *Courtesy of Garland County Historical Society*

a coincidence." Looking back through the years of the McLaughlin era, the magazine said that the city had settled into a "low, evil, up-all-night, bad-example setting and extremely comfortable life." The article stated that "Mayor Leo Patrick McLaughlin . . . presides over Hot Springs' delinquencies with a sharp eye and wondrous dignity that has an unfortunate tendency to splutter at critical moments. As Mayor, Mr. McLaughlin is official host to the gamblers, racketeers, hustlers, and other purveyors of the fast dollar who take asylum in his province and give Hot Springs its heady flavor." The magazine took aim at the mayor's conspicuously long term of office. "Some snide Hot Springers

Marine veteran Sid McMath, seen to the left, returned to his home town from the South Pacific determined to change the political picture of Hot Springs. McMath attacked Mayor McLaughlin's machine at its heart: the poll tax system. Against the odds McMath won the prosecuting attorney's post in 1946, but even with this post he could not get a conviction for corruption against the embattled mayor, who would retire conviction-free in 1948. The gambling shut down, but only for a short time, as McMath went on to be elected governor in 1948.

have insinuated that the people who count McLaughlin's votes have fif-teen fingers on each hand."

In describing the open gambling in the town, ranging from "the fashionable Belvedere and Tower Club, to small ramshackle joints" adjacent to the grand bathhouses, the reporter declared that the arrangement gives a general effect that Central Avenue "resembles nothing so much as a wedding of a German spa with an American frontier town." The article noted that "money from the North is loose and fast, and the play is heavy, whether it is roulette, craps, bingo or horses." The magazine also took aim at the mayor's claims of better-ing the city: "The Mayor's theory of better government involves the payment of fines at regular intervals by proprietors of the gambling halls." The reporter questioned whether or not the revenue had been used to improve the city, citing things like potholes in city streets. The article even revisited the issue of the mayor's removal of slot machines at the Army and Navy Hospital while he had allowed them elsewhere, even "in men's and ladies restrooms." The unkindest cut at the city, and this in an article that lacked any positives at all, came at the end of the piece. A doctor at the hospital had been asked to offer testimony on the healing powers of the thermal waters, and he declared, "Since I have been at the hospital we have been giving mineral baths to all our patients, and I can truthfully say that in all that time we have not had one case of smelly feet."[7]

Mayor McLaughlin's supporters quickly tried to pin blame for the negative publicity on Sid McMath and the GIs. Sid McMath and his band of GI reformers managed to get the issue of McLaughlin's bogus poll-tax votes into federal court, where the mayor lacked the influence he had over Garland County judges. The federal judge voided enough of McLaughlin's prepackaged votes, totaling some 1,600, to give Democrat Sid McMath a win in the prosecuting attorney's race. Though the rest of the GI slate had lost in the Democratic primary, they ran in November as independents and won their offices. Although McLaughlin himself was not up for re-election that year, almost all his supporters in other offices were swept out by the reformers, includ-ing the circuit judge, sheriff, county judge, and treasurer, on a record turnout of voters. An *Arkansas Democrat* editorial a few months after the election said, "The Garland County machine died hard. It was defeated only by a stout-hearted, uphill fight of the GI forces."[8]

A drunken hotel guest dozing off with a lit cigarette caused a fatal fire that destroyed the aging Great Northern Hotel despite the best efforts of Hot Springs firemen. The thirty-nine-year-old construction worker staying at the hotel admitted buying a six pack before collapsing into a drunken slumber with a lit cigarette. He escaped; another guest did not and burned to death. The hotel had accommodated budget conscious visitors since opening in 1897. Like a scene played out all too often in the history of Hot Springs, the dawn after the hotel fire revealed a shell of what had housed thousands of visitors over the preceding half century. *Courtesy of Garland County Historical Society*

Riding The Ducks
HOT SPRINGS, ARKANSAS
Amphibian Land & Lake Tours

World War II was over, but one of the tools that helped win it was adapted to become a permanent part of the Hot Springs tourist business. Former landing craft were converted to "ducks" that transported tourists around town and across parts of Lake Hamilton before their ride ended. The ducks still carry visitors today from offices on Central Avenue.

Concluding the most tumultuous political year in its history, Hot Springs ended 1946 reporting a record number of paying bathers, 1,042,000, more in one year than in all its history. In a single day that year, the Arlington Hotel marked on its books 750 baths and 500 massages. The jubilant bathing industry in Hot Springs did not realize, however, that the bathing phenomenon had peaked and would never see numbers like that again.

As 1947 got underway, with the GI reformers taking office, the fate of illegal gambling in Hot Springs hung in the balance, and most citizens expected it to finally end. Prosecuting attorney McMath would make arrests for money laundering, bribe-taking, and other crimes. The mayor was acquitted but opted not to stand for re-election, ending a twenty-year reign over Hot Springs.

With McMath as the prosecuting attorney, the open, large-scale gambling in Hot Springs was shut down, at least for a time. McMath would be elected governor in 1948 on the strength of his name recognition. However, he was replaced by a more gambling-friendly prosecuting attorney, and soon gambling was back in Hot Springs.

left: Some sought therapy with needle showers, in this case fired from across the room while the man stood in a stall with multiple directed shower heads. *Courtesy of Garland County Historical Society*

below: The peak of the bathing industry in Hot Springs was 1946, when for the first time the number of baths given topped one million. *Courtesy of Garland County Historical Society*

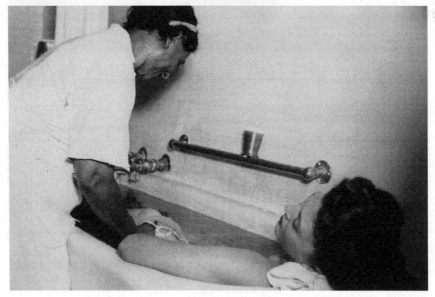

After a late-night raid in 1956 the state police photograph this line of slot machines beneath a "No Minors Allowed To Play" sign. That night nobody was playing in what would have otherwise been a packed gaming room. The raid was but a temporary interruption. The gambling, and the illegal sale of alcohol, would soon resume. *Courtesy of Garland County Historical Society*

The law enforcement raids, especially those by Garland County officers under political and media pressure, were reported to have ended with the complete destruction of the confiscated slot machines. As this April 1956 political cartoon from the *Arkansas Democrat* cleverly pointed out, the machines were rapidly repaired and often were back in service within days if not hours. *Courtesy of* Arkansas Democrat

CHAPTER ELEVEN

Changing Times
1950–1960

One of the most significant moments for Hot Springs in the 1950s was an event that would not be noted in the history books until decades later. In 1953 a young man named Roger Clinton arrived in Hot Springs, having moved from the city of Hope with his wife Virginia and her son, William Jefferson Blythe, whom Clinton later adopted. The boy was soon enrolled in St. John's Catholic School, where even the nuns who taught him would later predict that the little boy was "going to be president someday."[1]

In 1954 Gov. Francis Cherry, who had defeated Sid McMath in 1952, was running for a second two-year term. During his first term Cherry had been fairly aloof and indifferent to Hot Springs' gambling addiction. Still, according to Maxine Jones, the best-known brothel operator in the city, the business and gambling community opted to raise money for Cherry's challenger from the Ozarks, Orval E. Faubus. Writing in her autobiography, *Call Me Madam*, Jones called Faubus a "Governor of the People." She was well known in Hot Springs at the time, and according to her version she was invited to a meeting of the gambling and political leadership, which included a state senator, to help raise money for Faubus, based on his implied promise to let Hot Springs have its gambling if elected. On election day Jones loaned her Cadillac to a cab driver to use in transporting voters to the polls, including some of the prostitutes in her employ whom she had instructed to vote for Faubus in multiple polling places. It may be that such tactics contributed to his win, for Faubus scored an upset over Governor Cherry. Governor Faubus spent the next decade looking the other way, while gambling thrived in Hot Springs, bearing out the tale told by the madam about his commitment to the city.[2]

The *Arkansas Gazette* editorial page took a new tactic in attacking illegal gambling in Hot Springs, pointing out the evasion of income taxes. Still, in 1961 it was reported that as many as four hundred people were employed by the Hot Springs gambling clubs. *Courtesy of* Arkansas Gazette

Before the decade of the fifties was out, Hot Springs would gain a grand promenade, a broad landscaped sidewalk running the length of Bathhouse Row. However, the decade, coming on the heels of a record number of bathers in 1940s, would see a rapidly falling number of health seekers still believing in the healing power of the legendary thermal waters.

By the mid 1950s, with gambling-friendly Orval Faubus in the governor's office, Hot Springs was again a wide-open gambling city. The Tower Club on the Little Rock highway was one of the newer clubs packing its gaming tables nightly.

Mayor Leo McLaughlin, who ruled Hot Springs for twenty years, had been in retirement for a decade when he died at the age of sixty-seven. A few months after his death, rumors that he was buried with ill-gotten money prompted grave robbers to disinter him. *Courtesy of* Arkansas Democrat

A tourist draw that would delight thousands for many years, the IQ Zoo opened in 1955 on Whittington Avenue. The enterprise was the creation of industrial psychologist Keller Breland and his wife, Marian. They used behavioral principles to train chickens to dance, rabbits to play the piano, and raccoons to score at basketball.

CHAPTER TWELVE

The Last Roll of the Dice
1960–1970

In 1960 the Army and Navy Hospital was closed, something residents of Hot Springs had feared for decades. Peacetime and a more developed system of Veterans Administration hospitals had caused it to become unnecessary. The facility was transferred to the state for use as a rehabilitation center, softening the blow only slightly. Further cultural and economic shocks lay ahead in this decade, including the final chapter on illegal gambling.

Hot Springs still had gambling as a significant source of employment, and an article in the *Arkansas Gazette* in December 1960 put some numbers on the industry's impact. Under a headline, "Paper Says Rift May Shut Clubs at Hot Springs," the paper quoted the *Sentinel Record*, reporting that the casinos might have to close in early 1961 unless the "gamblers and other unidentified persons can work out an agreement as to how to divide the revenue." One source speculated that the friction was because of a syndicate who "was trying to gain a foothold in Hot Springs." The story said about four hundred people in the city were employed in the gambling business and that "amusement taxes" from the clubs collected by the city averaged $6,039 a month.[1]

The struggles over gambling in Hot Springs took a new, violent turn in early 1963 when a bomb exploded in the plush Vapors Supper Club on Park Avenue, doing $125,000 in damage but causing no injuries. Opinions widely varied on what would remain an unsolved crime. Unnamed local sources blamed it on an out-of-state syndicate intent on getting a piece of the gambling action in the city. The Cook County sheriff in Chicago, Richard Ogilvie, was asked if he thought gamblers were being crowded out of the northern city's underworld and trying to get into Hot Springs. Prior to the Vapors explosion,

Governor Orval Faubus was a frequent visitor to Hot Springs, having long espoused the view that gambling was a local issue and not a state concern. As he was nearing the end of his twelve years in office, for which he was paid ten thousand dollars a year, he built an expensive home atop a mountain in Huntsville, saying his "friends" helped him pay for it. That those friends included the Hot Springs gamblers was long suspected but never proven. In this photograph circa 1962 he visits with a representative of the chamber of commerce. *Courtesy of Garland County Historical Society*

Chicago had experienced a series of mystery fires in some of its own shady nightspots. The northern sheriff allowed that it was certainly possible, scoffing at Hot Springs' claim that its gambling industry was home owned and operated. He then launched an attack on Arkansas's Senator John McClellan, currently investigating gangland activity. "Nonsense," the sheriff said, questioning what he considered to be McClellan's selective attacks on organized crime. "One of the great enigmas to me is how McClellan can do such a great job in the rest of the country and leave that place alone."[2]

While Hot Springs still earned revenue from its illicit gambling, its legal offering, the thermal baths, was a lagging business by 1963. Hot Springs was hosting a record number of visitors, but most were not coming to bathe. The National Park Service reported that for the year prior, only 478,788 baths had been given, down markedly from the peak year of 1946 when just over one million baths were sold. Officials and business people around town attempted to offer explanations about the decline. Some blamed modern medicine, miracle drugs, and the hard-to-admit truth that far fewer people put faith in the medicinal power of the waters than did past generations. Some, whose profits were tied to bathing, even blamed Hot Springs' nightlife and illicit gambling for pulling visitors away from the bathhouses.

Writing for the *Arkansas Gazette* in 1991, journalist Bob Lancaster, in an essay entitled "Cosmopolitan Oasis," looked back at the late 1950s and early 1960s in Hot Springs and the decline of the bathing industry, which by then was an admission of reality by even the most die-hard believers in the powers of the thermal waters to make the city a destination. "But if you grew up in Arkansas before the mid 1960s, the unique influence of that little piece of street [Central Avenue] probably touched you. It made you aware that there were professional palm readers in the world—your world, and professional 'colonic irrigators.' And curbside hot tamale vendors. And people who *lived* in hotels. And brothel madams who showed their wares in convertibles in traditional municipal parades." Lancaster went on to explain why by the 1960s the bathing industry was fast fading. "The advent of penicillin and antibiotics. The automobile killed the passenger train and the new mode of transportation disrupted the ritual and regimen of resort bathing. With the baby boom, most people's holidays involved children and the baths had never been something that got along with kids. . . . After a time, Hot Springs started looking elsewhere for its future and grew off in other directions, away from Central Avenue and the Diocletian baths."[3]

By 1964 newspapers outside the central Arkansas area were beginning to take shots at Hot Springs' illicit gambling in their editorial pages. The *News Observer* of Crossett, Arkansas, took aim on March 8, 1964:

> There have been all kinds of theories advanced as to why the paradox of Hot Springs is allowed to exist in a normal law abiding, Bible reading, church going state such as Arkansas. Some suggest it is because the people don't actually know what is going on. Hog

wash. The Hot Springs story has been told more often than Mother Goose—and believed just about as often. Others say it is because the pay-off to the politicians is so great, no one can stop it. Again we say Hog Wash. The people can stop any political payoff they want by just going to the polls and voting. . . . It has also been hinted that maybe the reason Hot Springs is like it is, is because that's the way the people really want it. Maybe the people of Arkansas like to gamble. Maybe they like to go night clubbing. Maybe they like to do a little sinning. We are sure they do, but they don't want to do it at home. They don't want to gamble in front of their own children or neighbors. The don't like the idea of local night clubs and local sin-spots, but they see little, if any, harm, in having them in Garland County. . . . We think this theory holds water. . . . Perhaps this is good. We won't judge. Perhaps even the best man is part hypocrite. We don't know. What is plain is that in present day Arkansas we have a double-standard of law enforcement in operation that should give pause to even the most hardened crap-shooter or horse follower. It is a standard in which no pride can be taken, because if today it only affects gambling, who is to say what it will affect tomorrow?[4]

Far from the small town of Crossett, Arkansas, the *New York Daily News* also focused on Hot Springs' gambling addiction in March 1964, with a headline calling the city the "Biggest Non-Floating Dice Game." The paper was drawn to the story after learning that the Justice Department was investigating illegal gambling in the city, quoting the chief of the department's organized crime section, William Hunley, as saying the city had the biggest illegal gambling operation in the nation. The paper, in a two-part exposé, had learned that the federal jurisdiction was in play because of suspected violations of a federal law that made it illegal to move gambling equipment or personnel across state lines. The *Daily News* also took a slap at Sen. John L. McClellan, who had been making headlines in Washington DC through his hearings looking into organized crime in primarily northern cities. The New York reporter got out his atlas and pointed out to readers that "Hot Springs is only 64 miles from Camden, Arkansas, the home of Senator John L. McClellan himself." Gov. Orval Faubus, when asked for comment on the series, accused the Justice Department of trying to make headlines in its campaign to slow down or halt the Hot Springs casinos. The reporter summarized the

Despite renewed gambling, Hot Springs was unable to generate interest or money to save its 1880s-era opera house on Central Avenue, which fell to the wreckers ball.

Not long after the opera house was demolished, the Rock Island train depot, originally built for Diamond Joe Reynolds's narrow-gauge train, was razed to make way for a new convention center. Outgoing mayor Floyd Housely steered through a city ordinance taxing illegal gambling to raise money for the new center. Large casinos were taxed $500 a month, smaller ones $200, slot machines $5, and bingo parlors $50. *Courtesy of Garland County Historical Society*

governor's position to be that casinos are a local issue and for that reason he had not intervened in almost a decade of holding the governor's office.[5]

In March the Arkansas House of Representatives adopted a resolution by a ninety-one-to-three margin (with only the Garland County legislators opposing) calling on local law enforcement in Hot Springs to shut down the illegal gambling. It furnished an excuse for Faubus to take action, and the headlines on March 28, 1964, read, "Faubus Orders Doors of Casinos Closed; Police Will Comply." By midnight most of the casinos had shut down on their own in advance of the police enforcement. It was the first meaningful interruption in gambling since the administration of Governor McMath in 1947–48. The economic blow for Garland County was forecast to be painful, with an estimated nine hundred people who would lose their jobs in an industry that federal sources estimated was taking in $50 million a year.[6]

Throughout the summer of 1964, the gambling interests in Hot Springs were determined not to give up the lucrative enterprise that had become ingrained into the city. The business community set about to wage at least one last fight, and this time an actual legal fight. Garland County officials set about to get a ballot initiative set for a statewide vote in November 1964 to allow legal casinos in Hot Springs. One of the biggest boosters of the initiative was Dane Harris, operator of the Vapors Supper Club and the Belvedere Club.

A reporter from the *Arkansas Gazette* visited the Vapors to interview Dane Harris a week after most of the casinos had shut down, in the wake of Governor Faubus's reluctant order. Harris claimed that the Vapors was so modern it even had "a refrigerated garbage room." Harris passionately espoused the view that gambling was actually good for Arkansas's image. "This gambling industry has become a way of life here. It's like a grocery store, it has benefited directly or indirectly everybody in Hot Springs." Harris told the reporter that, between his interest in the Vapors and the Belvedere, he employed 550 people, which would have made him one of the largest employers in Hot Springs at the time. He was clearly using the occasion to win support for the coming initiative to legalize gambling in the city. "It would clearly be a tremendous thing not only for Garland County but the state of Arkansas—if the bill is properly written. By this I mean that if it has the proper controls, and puts the business in the hands of capable people, is local and is on a high plane. It should be restricted to the number of places—it shouldn't be open to every filling station operator like in Nevada."[7]

With its casinos idle, Hot Springs wasted no time in pushing the effort to legalize the industry. Petitions were circulating by the middle of April, seeking 35,000 signatures to get the initiative on the November 1964 ballot. The intent was to give Hot Springs the right to have a local referendum and not have the question decided by a statewide vote. To placate critics who feared the city would take on a sprawling Las Vegas look, the proposal stipulated that no more than one casino could operate for each 7,000 residents of Garland County and that any casino operator must have lived in Arkansas for the preceding twenty years. By June the Hot Springs Chamber of Commerce presented the secretary of state with almost 75,000 signatures, double the number needed to get the question on the ballot; if enacted, it would have become Amendment 55 to the state's 1874 constitution.

As the gambling-free summer of 1964 dragged on, loud bewailing of economic woe steadily came of out Hot Springs. The Southern Grill (and casino) across the street from the Arlington shut down in July, closing even its bar and liquor store. The owner said he could not break even on the greatly reduced number of patrons, and he told reporters he would stay closed until he saw the outcome of the gambling ballot initiative in the fall. The Vapors said it also was near closing, along with several other nightspots.[8]

The Vapors' Dane Harris drew the attention of the *Saturday Evening Post* in September 1964. The headline read "Showdown in Arkansas: No Dice in Hot Springs." The article offered a remarkable insight in the gamblers' civic-minded efforts, as they saw them, to showcase legalized gambling as good for Hot Springs and for the state as a whole. Sometimes tongue in cheek, sometimes in all seriousness, the writer shared the story of the constitutional-amendment campaign with the nation.

> Civic virtue is not the first thing that leaps to mind at the mention of Hot Springs, Ark, a sedately sinful little resort town in the Ouachita Mountains. But this election year Hot Springs citizens are taking a public-spirited interest in the campaign.
> It must be added however, the word "campaign" in Hot Springs has nothing to do with the activities of Lyndon Johnson

and Barry Goldwater, not with those of Gov. Orval Faubus and his Republican opponent, Winthrop Rockefeller. "Campaign" means how to get the craps tables at the Vapors and the Southern Club going again before everyone starves to death from a lack of hundred dollar bills. It is hoped that something called the "Lawful Wagering Act Amendment" will accomplish this. It had better. Hundred dollar bills are very important to Hot Springs, which prides itself on being a green-money town, as distinct from Las Vegas, where a hatful of silver dollars makes you a sport. . . .

Just now, however, Hot Springs is a disaster area. A hotel man with nothing but clean sheets on his hands struggled a few days ago to express the horror of the situation: "You can't get into a friendly poker game," he said gloomily. His voice gathered force. "I mean, there aren't even any punchboards."

This is appalling news. Until a few months ago Hot Springs had been green as an elegant oasis for those who enjoyed gracious wagering almost without a break since the Civil War.

The writer quoted William G. Hundley, chief of the Justice Department's Organized Crime and Racketeering Section, who had called Hot Springs the nation's largest illegal gambling mecca. This led someone else to add, without being named, that "no matter how careful they were back home the vacationing dentists who took their wives to Hot Springs handled their lizard-skin wallets like oilmen. Cracking off crunchy new bills from their neat packets of saved up hundreds was part of the cure they came for, like the mineral baths."

The *Post* writer found local citizens widely supporting the gambling amendment in part because Hot Springs mayor Dan Wolf had plans to build a new city hall with the amusement taxes to be levied on the legal gambling.

The article illustrated also the changing demographics of Hot Springs visitors.

What had been a convenience for the visiting mineral bathers and horse players had became the tourist town's main tourist trap. The lavish old Arlington Hotel, an enormous pile whose mineral baths had poached the gimpy rich profitably for decades, suddenly found that it had competition from a set of flashy new motels whose guests bathed only when their necks got dirty. The ancient Southern Club packed its oldest established craps tables three-deep with solvent optimists.

The *Saturday Evening Post* located Dane Harris, reporting that he arrived in 1959 already prosperous from gambling where it had been legal. "With some friends, also local, he built a casino and supper club called the Vapors, on a scale only slightly less grand than that of the Las Vegas pleasure domes."

Harris and the other casinos had, according to the *Post*, given generously back to the community. "The casino owners joined the Chamber of Commerce and built two free swimming pools for the city, one white, one colored. Gambling money, in one tactful way or the other, was contributed to church fund drives." Harris, in his interview, was most passionate in defense of his business. "We are respected, there's no feeling that we are doing something unlawful."

The magazine found a witty rebuttal to Harris in the form of Rev. J. N. Harrison of the town's Union Baptist Church: "Just because they've been gambling here for a hundred years doesn't make it right. They've been robbing banks a long time too."

The magazine piece closed with some speculation on whether or not the amendment would pass in the fall, and ended with some biting final comments: "There was a time when you could find cynics who thought the city fathers of Hot Springs did not really want legal gambling. (Would the tourists find it as spicy? Would the graft grow as green?) Now it is legal or bust, and this unrepentant little resort is fighting for its low, evil, up-all night, bad-example-setting and extremely comfortable life."[9]

Arkansas voters went to the polls on November 4, 1964, and re-elected Orval Faubus to a sixth term over Winthrop Rockefeller. The vote that mattered most to Hot Springs, however, was on the question of giving Garland County the right to have a local option election on casinos. The clouds of disappointment were deep and dark over places like the Vapors and the Southern Club, for by a margin of 318,229 to 215,744 the voters of Arkansas said no to the question. The ballot initiative only carried in four of seventy-five counties, though it won in Garland County by a three-to-one margin. The disappointed Hot Springs Chamber of Commerce spokesman only stated, "Now we are busy with our new plans for the future of the city."[10]

Was gambling finally ended in Hot Springs? It seemed like a good bet, but Governor Faubus's response to the balloting the day after the election probably should have been examined closely. He said it would now be "impossible for casinos to operate openly. Of course, you can't stop back room gambling but I'm going to use the police power of the state to prevent open casino gambling."[11]

In December, after the defeat of the gambling ballot effort, a headline in the *Arkansas Democrat* noted that, "Big Spenders Bypass Law-Abiding Resort." "All the one-armed bandits stand like prisoners of war in a corner of the Vapors, their three eyes staring into the darkness. All over town thousands of dry martini glasses glisten behind unpeopled bars. The action is gone. The party is over. At least for a while. . . . The plush restaurants are serving fried chicken and $3 steaks instead of exotic dishes and $8 steaks." The story the reporter kept hearing was that Hot Springs had to rebuild into a more traditional, family-oriented tourist business, to "adjust away from the Cadillac trade back to the family trade." The challenge was clear: "The most important thing to do is give the tourists something to do at night."[12]

Governor Faubus had parsed his words more closely than many people had noticed after the election, pledging to keep open casino gambling shut down but adding that, in his view, nothing could be done about "backroom gambling." Club operators took this as license to creatively bypass the letter of the law, and by 1965 the casinos were running again but this time under the guise of "private clubs." Memberships to these clubs was not hard to come by, as long as the doorkeeper decided the new member was not an undercover policeman.

Gambling-related bombings had made headlines in 1963 and hit the news again on April 1, 1965. Dane Harris, the owner and operator of the Vapors Supper Club, which had been bombed two years earlier, found the violence striking close to home, very close. Late at night, a bomb went off in the garage at Harris's home, damaging four automobiles, one a Lincoln Continental. The bombers would strike again that same night, this time at the home of circuit judge P. E. Dobbs, an important political figure in Garland County; a bomb exploded under his 1964 Rambler automobile. The bombings, whose perpetrators were unknown, sent shockwaves through the town, and especially through the tourist business community. "This kind of publicity can absolutely ruin a resort area," was the message from the chamber of commerce. A gangland stigma was the most widely voiced concern. Others had a different message and concerns. James Gannaway was a Little Rock lawyer working on behalf of Churches United Against Gambling, whose response was that "those who play with fire get burned." Gannaway was critical of the local law enforcement for pledging to work twenty-four hours a day to find the bomber when they had been not nearly as diligent at enforcing laws against gambling. "Crime breeds crime, you can't pamper, harbor criminals and hoodlums without breeding an ever larger criminal community."[13]

Winthrop Rockefeller launched his second run for the governor's office in 1966 when Orval Faubus chose not to seek re-election after six terms. Gambling was a topic in the election, and Rockefeller's position was that he was morally opposed to gambling and, even more so, the hypocrisy of allowing it while the voters of the state had made it clear they did not want it legalized. Rockefeller won the November election, becoming the first Republican governor in a century for the state. The gamblers were nervous, but they had survived many politicians' promises to enforce the law in the past. Maybe Rockefeller would not be much different, they hoped. Hope was in vain, as it turned out.

The Little Rock press was considerably more interested in the gambling issue in Hot Springs than in past decades, and they were also evaluating what the new governor would do. The *Arkansas Democrat* found, among other things, twenty-one gaming tables and seven slot machines running in the Ohio Club. In the plush Vapors, the reporter found "it was virtually impossible to get a table to see Mickey Rooney at the Vapors and its casino was so over crowded that 'expectant gamblers' were being referred to the White Front Club."[14]

The Arkansas Legislature, in session during the spring of 1967, did what they had failed to do in attempts of 1957 and 1959: they passed a bill to legalize gambling in Hot Springs, restricted to four unidentified clubs. It was a challenge of sorts from the overwhelming Democratic legislature to the Republican governor. Shortly before the bill was to become law without the governor's signature, Rockefeller vetoed the legislation. Hot Springs had come as close as it likely ever would to gaining legalized casino gambling, and it had fallen short.

For a time, the gamblers shrugged off the legislative defeat and tried to stay in business, but it was not to be. Unlike past governors, Win Rockefeller followed through on his promise to bring casino gambling to an end.

The almost century-long affair with illegal gambling in Hot Springs finally came to an end in 1967 under orders given to the state police by new governor Winthrop Rockefeller. Slot machines and other gambling equipment was loaded up and taken to the dump, crushed and burned. Efforts would surface in later years to legalize casino gambling, but all have failed thus far. *Courtesy of Garland County Historical Society*

CHAPTER THIRTEEN

The Spa City in Its Postgambling Era
1970–1990

The *Arkansas Gazette,* which had long rejected the claim that Hot Springs could not prosper without gambling, offered an editorial on February 5, 1974, entitled, "'The Spa' in Winter." It proposed that "just ahead of the racing season may be the best time to visit Hot Springs, which is or ought to be everybody's favorite resort. . . . In Hot Springs one can still capture downtown the elusive feeling, as in one of those Rod Serling TV stories, of a place that hasn't changed in 50 years and, by the grace of God, won't change in 50 more."[1] The wistful editorialist conveniently overlooked the fact that for much of the preceding fifty years Hot Springs had been the nation's foremost illegal gambling mecca, among other vices not to be found there in the winter of 1974. In a bit of a mockery of the editorialist's musings, the storied Maurice Bathhouse closed down before the end of 1974, for the bathers just did not come anymore.

By February 1975 Bathhouse Row was a shadow of its former glory, with two of the bathhouses shuttered. However a faint pulse still beat, as a headline read, "Hot Springs Bathhouse Row Called 'One of Finest Remaining in Nation.'" The entire row was added to the roster of the National Register of Historic Places. It was envisioned that the federal designation would open up funding options and create interest in finding alternative uses for the shuttered bathhouses. The Fordyce had been closed since 1962, and one by one the other proud bathhouses on the row would follow the Maurice into retirement: the Ozark in 1977, the Hale in 1978, the Superior in 1983 (only one month shy of its hundredth year in business, though in two different buildings), the Quapaw in 1984, and the Lamar in 1985.

While the bathing business continued a steady decline, there was a bright spot to boost tourism. Inspired in 1971 by actions of the

When gambling ended, Hot Springs worked to develop family-oriented attractions, one being the Josephine Tussaud Wax Museum, housed in the former gambling palace, the Southern Club.

Arkansas legislature, the Mid-America Science Museum was launched with state funding. It would be 1979 before the Smithsonian Institution–affiliated museum opened. Today the museum operates about a hundred interactive exhibits in a multimillion-dollar campus west of the city.

As the 1980s opened, news articles appeared from time to time, taking the city's pulse during an increasingly lengthy gambling-free era. *Arkansas Gazette* journalist Doug Smith paid a visit in 1980 and wrote an article headlined, "Who Says Nobody Goes to Hot Springs Anymore?" Smith found the visitors that did come were no longer "high rollers, not real big spenders, probably people who aren't ashamed of being both Arkansans and tourists, and who think Hot Springs is a good place to get away from their daily grind." Brunch in the lobby of the Arlington seemed popular, but there were some complaints from visitors that the night life was not what it once was. "It's hard to find a nice, quite cocktail lounge anymore. They're all go-go

Hill Wheatley, who would live to be an active ninety-nine, owned much of downtown Hot Springs. He donated the Gaines block, near the federal courthouse, for conversion to a park. Sadly, the project would doom an entire block of historic buildings to the wrecking ball, including the Greek-revival-style Arkansas Trust Company building. *Courtesy of Butler Center for Arkansas Studies*

this page and opposite: Almost a century after fire destroyed much of Hot Springs, it returned to claim one more hotel in 1975: the Moody, which had been rebuilt after the 1913 fire. It was the third and last Moody Hotel to sit on the site. *Courtesy of Garland County Historical Society*

places or strip joints now. My wife and I went to the Black Orchid and we ran into a topless dancer just inside the door. My wife said it was like looking at two headlights."[2]

The desire on the part of some people to see Hot Springs revived to some semblance of its former glory sometimes got a bit far into the rumor mill. Such was the headline in 1983 above a story explaining that no, Frank Sinatra was *not* buying the Arlington Hotel. A cab driver had started the rumor, and it got around quickly.

Hot Springs residents enjoyed praise in *W* magazine in January 1987. "Hot Springs Beats Paris for Jet Set," read the headline of an article that astonished some city officials. "It has been 60 years since George Raft and Al Capone strolled the streets of Hot Springs but now, in 1987, the town is 'in' again for the fashionable jet set." The article bore companion photographs of the Eiffel Tower and the Hot Springs Mountain Tower, and the magazine reported that people again had come to prefer quiet resort towns that were pleasant and not hard to get to, though the author admitted Hot Springs was "hardly Paree."[3] The magazine was said to have a worldwide circulation of 300,000.

The ever-present wrecking ball, aided by controlled demolition, continued its march through historic Hot Springs in 1976, taking the Tiffany-brick-encased COMO Hotel to make way for yet another bank. The hotel, boarded up and closed since 1965, had graced the intersection since 1934. *Courtesy of Garland County Historical Society*

Hot Springs city fathers, always looking for some way to increase the number of visitors, were thinking outside the box by 1992. A change in the federal designation of the Hot Springs National Park might have allowed larger, different developments if, for instance, it became a national monument instead of a national park. One idea originally proposed in the 1980s was described in the *Arkansas Gazette:* "Hot Springs officials have been talking of constructing monorails and sky rides and building a cascade of hot water tumbling from the mountain into a pool." These ideas were soon discarded, however, and the national park designation was retained.

One of Hot Springs most successful and acclaimed accomplishments in the post-gambling era was the establishment of the Hot Springs Documentary Film Festival, which each fall for a decade has drawn crowds and independent films from around the world.

CHAPTER FOURTEEN

Bringing a World-Renowned
Resort to a Crossroads
1991 to the Present

Hot Springs, in an almost constant stage of reinvention since its wilderness founding, continues to move ahead today while working to retain a link to its history and its natural gifts.

"There's a magic here that hasn't happened since SoHo in the 1960s, Santa Fe in the 1970s. Where will it be in the 90s? It might as well be here." These words were those of an unidentified observer commenting on the conversion of vacant storefronts to art galleries on the southern end of the Central Avenue historic district—an idea that had finally taken hold. During the decades before the 1960s a staple of Central Avenue had been art auctions that drew crowds to bid on art treasures. The novelty had long faded for such attractions. In the fall of 1993, however, select evenings found as many as twenty art galleries lit up and welcoming strollers to see paintings, handsome wooden turned bowls, and other creative works. The artists had been trickling in since the late 1980s, and as their endeavors took hold, they began to buy and improve the buildings that housed their galleries. Hot Springs and a growing number of visitors and serious art patrons all began to take notice. Said one gallery owner, "Hot Springs doesn't have the usual tourist attractions; it's not Disneyland. . . . We've got the baths, the lakes, the mountains and now the art."[1]

In April 2002 Hot Springs hosted a grand opening of what would soon become one of its most popular draws outside of the historic downtown: the Garvan Woodland Gardens. The attraction's roots went back to 1955 when Verna Cook Garvan visited the undeveloped peninsula on Lake Hamilton that she had inherited. The land had belonged to her father, Arthur Cook, who had grown wealthy from

NATIONAL BAPTIST SANITARIUM-BATH HOUSE
501 MALVERN AVENUE   HOT SPRINGS NATIONAL PARK, ARKANSAS
TELEPHONE 5656

Originally called the Woodmen of the Union building when built in 1922, the National
Baptist Hotel and Bathhouse was the first-class black hotel in the city for many years.
Count Basie and Joe Lewis were counted among its entertainers and guests over the
years. Once the heart of the black-entertainment and business district of the city, it was
fated for demolition, decayed, and abandoned. In a rare success story, it has been rescued and is being restored for a multipurpose development.

his Wisconsin-Arkansas Lumber Company and Malvern Brick & Tile.
He died in an automobile accident when Verna was only twenty-two
and left her to run the family business empire. Mrs. Garvan set out
with a dream to develop a great garden on the site, a world-class
botanical garden for the enjoyment of all the people of the state. The
first structures were designed under commission by famed architects
E. Fay Jones and Maurice Jennings. By 1985 Garvin had signed a trust
agreement for the land with the University of Arkansas and its School
of Architecture. The university inherited the property in 1993 upon
Garvan's death, and large-scale development of the gardens started in
2000. Today the gardens host weddings and other special occasions
and showcase a large-scale light show at Christmas, drawing thousands of visitors.

Hot Springs, throughout its history, possessed among its people
those whose views were often at odds with the rest of the state, and
the rest of the state often just shrugged, for it was Hot Springs after

all. Steve Arrison, executive director of the Hot Springs Advertising and Promotion Commission, experienced this attitude first hand in September 2003 when he sought to put Abraham Lincoln on display in the city's convention center. Decades before, wealthy Chicago visitor Benjamin Kulp had gifted the city with a rare bronze scale model of a seated Lincoln, which had been used to design the Lincoln Memorial in Washington DC in the 1920s. Arrison had found the valuable statue in storage, where it had sat in obscurity for forty years, and announced his intent to display it, assuming no one would object. However, the local chapter of the Sons of Confederate Veterans did object, vehemently proclaiming that Lincoln had waged war on the South and that "having an exhibition anywhere in Dixie of this depraved thug is the equivalent of having a statue of Adolph Hitler in Israel." Still, the statue was cleaned up and put on display, despite the hundreds of letters and e-mails received that were reportedly against the idea.[2]

"Deciding What's Hot in Spa City" was the *Arkansas Democrat-Gazette* headline in September 2004. The following article described a city hanging in the balance between its storied history and its potential as a future tourist draw. On Bathhouse Row only a single bathhouse was operational: the Buckstaff. One businessman interviewed referred to visitors as doing the "bathhouse shuffle." Strollers on Central Avenue would walk up to one of the fabled bathhouses, like the Ozark or Quapaw, only to find locked doors and empty rooms when they peered through the windows.[3]

Hot Springs had been born as a fabled spa resort early in the nineteenth century, and then came to depend on gambling revenue for over eight decades. Ironically, as the twenty-first century got underway it was competing for visitor dollars with legal gambling in most of the adjoining states, in some cases only a river bridge away. The *Democrat-Gazette* reporter roamed the city, seeking to hear people's ideas about how to revive the city as a tourist destination. Some promoted the concept of a large outdoor thermal pool on the hillside for outdoor bathing. The owner of a downtown entertainment revue called *The Bath House Show* suggested perhaps a new city nickname or slogan instead of the old one: "We Bathe The World." Hot Springs could become, he said, "The Magical Springdom," playing off both the springs and the nearby Magic Springs theme park. Yet, the subject inevitably came back to

Hot Springs High School's best-known graduate returned to campaign for governor in 1982, when he would reclaim the office he lost two years earlier to Frank White. The future president moved to Hot Springs from Hope at the age of four, later graduating from high school in the spa city. *Courtesy of Garland County Historical Society*

gambling and the goal of some to finally win the right to have legal casinos that could compete with those in Mississippi, Missouri, Louisiana, and Oklahoma. The acknowledged reality, however, is that it would take statewide passage of an enabling constitutional amendment to allow the casinos again, and that is not considered likely.

Overall, the *Democrat-Gazette* article did find people upbeat or happy over the new convention center and its adjacent Embassy Suites Hotel complex. Perhaps Kenneth Wheatley III, whose family still owns about half of the historic buildings in the downtown area, said it best of the city, "We may need a stent or two, but we don't need surgery."

Hot Springs, where a fabled resort of healing waters sprang from the nineteenth-century frontier, entered the twenty-first century seeking to capitalize on its past while making its future. It has become a family destination, with three lakes, a theme park, a thriving art-gallery scene, an acclaimed film festival, fine dining, and a variety of entertainment, including the century-old alligator farm and a wax museum now housed in the old Southern Club, which for decades had been a thriving casino.

Hot Springs retains one legal gambling industry with a popular spring Oaklawn racing season. In recent years the racetrack won the right to simulcast horseraces from other tracks around the nation. Oaklawn also today offers video gaming.

Any discussion of the future of Hot Springs gravitates back to its past, and the face of its past, Bathhouse Row. The Fordyce Bathhouse, proudly restored, crowns the row as the headquarters and visitors center for Hot Springs National Park. The National Park Service invested substantial sums in restoring the rest of the bathhouses with the goal to see them leased for tourist-oriented commercial enterprises, though not likely to be used any longer for bathing. A bright exception was the restored Quapaw Bathhouse, which reopened for bathing in 2009.

Beyond the Bathhouse Row, the greatest challenge may be preserving the remainder of the buildings within the Central Avenue Historic District. Many are vacant above the street level today, including the towering Medical Arts Building and the Dugan Stuart Building. Their fate could well hinge on a successful leasing of the long-vacant bathhouses that may bring more people downtown, some, hopefully, to live and work.

This work closes with an image of one of the spa city's most battered survivors, the hundred-year-old Knickerbocker Hotel on Prospect Avenue, a short distance off of Central Avenue. Once slated for demolition, it stands today secured from the elements and awaiting a buyer to restore it so that it can once again welcome guests to the "Valley of the Vapors."

A then-and-now of the Knickerbocker Hotel, which opened in 1906. Boarded up and decaying for years—and but days from the wreckers ball—the hotel was saved by dedicated individuals who had a vision for a future restoration of the little hotel that symbolized much of the modest history of what was often called the "City of Visitors."

NOTES

CHAPTER ONE

1. Thomas Nutall, as quoted in *The Record*, Trey Berry, Garland County Historical Society, 2004, 20.

2. *The Record*, 21.

CHAPTER TWO

1. Thomas Nutall, as quoted in Francis J. Scully, *Hot Springs, Arkansas, and Hot Springs National Park* (Little Rock: Pioneer Press, 1966), 24.

2. "The Hot Springs," *Arkansas Gazette*, August 8, 1829.

3. Scully, 31–32.

4. *Arkansas Gazette*, February 4, 1834.

5. Hiram Whittington, as quoted in Scully, 28–29.

6. George W. Featherstonhaugh, as quoted in Scully, 29.

7. "US Postcoach Line from Little Rock to Hot Springs," *Arkansas Gazette*, June 27, 1838.

8. *Arkansas Gazette*, July 10, 1844.

9. "Religion in the Arkansas Wilderness," *Spirit of the Times* (New York, NY), July 1848, 12.

10. "A Banner Year at the Springs," *Arkansas True Democrat* (Little Rock), May 8, 1854, 1.

11. "News from the Springs," *Arkansas Gazette*, June 12, 1854.

12. *Arkansas True Democrat*, June 8, 1857, 2.

13. "A Grand Celebration at Hot Springs," *Arkansas Gazette*, July 5, 1859.

CHAPTER THREE

1. Dallas T. Herndon, *Centennial History of Arkansas* (Chicago and Little Rock: S. J. Clarke Publishing Company, 1922), 868.

2. "A Woman's View of Hot Springs in 1867," *Arkansas Gazette*, October 30, 1949.

3. "1876 Expedition to Arkansas," *Arkansas Gazette*, September 10, 1950.

4. Scully, 68–69.

5. Van Cleaf, *Harper's Monthly Magazine*, February 1878, 42–63.

6. As quoted in Van Cleaf, 79.

7. Dee Brown, *The American Spa* (Little Rock: Rose Publishing Company, 1982), 22.

8. As quoted in Van Cleaf, 81.

9. "A City in Ruin," *The Hot Springs Illustrated Monthly News* (AR), March 6, 1878, 1.

10. Hot Springs City Council Minutes, March 1879.
11. *The Hot Springs Illustrated Monthly News*, February 1, 1878.

CHAPTER FOUR

1. Herndon, 868.
2. Cutter, 42.
3. Cutter, 47.
4. Cutter, 48.
5. Cutter, 37
6. Orval E. Allbritton, *Hot Springs Gunsmoke*, (Hot Springs, AR: Garland County Historical Society, 2006), 72.
7. *Ye Hot Springs Arkansas Picture Book* (St. Louis: Woodward & Tiernan Printing Company, 1894), 15.

CHAPTER FIVE

1. "Hot Springs, the World's Greatest Health Resort," *Hot Springs Daily News* (AR), May 18, 1893.
2. *Ye Hot Springs*, 13.
3. "The Hot Springs of Arkansas, a World Class Resort," *Chicago Journal of Topics*, January 1893, 3.
4. *Ye Hot Springs*, 28–32.
5. "Deadly Day on Central Avenue," *Hot Springs Daily News*, March 17, 1899.
6. Mamie Ruth Abernathy, *History of Hot Springs*, 32.

CHAPTER SIX

1. Herndon, 868.
2. "Testimonials to Healing," *Hot Springs Herald* (AR), February 1901.
3. "Testimonials of Cures at Hot Springs," *The 400* (Chicago, IL), February 1893, 2.
4. Cutter, 41.
5. "Gone to Extremes," *Hot Springs Daily News*, June 9, 1903.
6. John C. Paige and Laura Harrison, *Out of the Vapors: A Social and Architectural History of Bathhouse Row* (Washington DC: U.S. Government Printing Office, 1987), 162.
7. "City in Ruins," *Sentinel Record*, February 26, 1905.
8. Sculley, 132.
9. "Airship Soars," *Sentinel Record*.
10. Orval Allbritton, *Leo and Verne: The Spa's Heyday* (Hot Springs, AR: Garland County Historical Society, 2004), 82.

CHAPTER SEVEN

1. Herndon, 868.
2. Paige and Harrison, 135.
3. Paige and Harrison, 137.
4. Paige and Harrison, 132.
5. Cutter, 34.
6. Cutter, 35.
7. *Sentinel Record*, June 18, 1912.
8. *Sentinel Record*, September 18, 1912.
9. *Evening Times* (Grand Forks, ND), July 24, 1911.
10. Allbritton, *Leo and Verne*, 61–64.
11. Allbritton, *Leo and Verne*, 61–64.
12. Orval Allbritton, 156.
13. Orval Allbritton, 158.
14. "Heavy Toll of the Fire Fiend," *Hot Springs Sentinel Record* (AR), September 6, 1913.
15. "Heavy Toll," *Sentinel Record*.
16. Allbritton, *Leo and Verne*, 61–64.
17. Cutter, 35.
18. Orval Allbritton, 61–62.
19. Orval Allbritton, 152.
20. Orval Allbritton, 82.

CHAPTER EIGHT

1. "Two Dead in Derailment," *Hot Springs Sentinel Record* (AR), February 11, 1921.
2. *Sentinel Record*, August 1, 1922.
3. *The Record*, 45.
4. Paige and Harrison, 142.
5. Peter Flournoy, ed., *The Torrid Twenties* (Hot Springs, AR: Junior Chamber of Commerce Auxiliary, 1951), 47.
6. *The Torrid Twenties*, 50.
7. *The Torrid Twenties*, 48.
8. Scully, 184.
9. "Ages Moonshiner Completes Final Sentence Today," *Hot Springs Sentinel Record* (AR), September 11, 1926.
10. Orval Allbritton, *Leo and Verne*, 156.
11. *The Record*, 137–38.

CHAPTER NINE

1. "Hot Springs' Birthday," *Sentinel Record*, June 22, 1932.
2. "Why Do Gangsters Like Hot Springs," *Public Opinion* (Hot Springs, AR), May 13, 1933, 3.
3. Walter Davenport, *Collier's Weekly*, August 8, 1931, 42–50.
4. *Public Opinion*, September 29, 1933.

5. "Roosevelt Stresses Broad Purpose of Constitution," *Public Opinion*, June 11, 1936.

6. "Hill Dwellers among Thousands Here to See FDR," *Sentinel Record*, June 11, 1936.

7. Allbritton, *Leo and Vern*, 410.

CHAPTER TEN

1. Justia.com, US Supreme Court Center, *Mitchell v. United States*.

2. Allbritton, *Leo and Verne*, 410.

3. Allbritton, *Leo and Verne*, 447.

4. U.S. Army Redistribution Manual (Hot Springs: U.S. Army, 1944), 2–3.

5. Allbritton, *Leo and Verne*, 460.

6. Allbritton, *Leo and Verne*, 464.

7. "Town without a Lid," *Saturday Evening Post*, July 20, 1946, 42–54.

8. "Machine Dies Hard," *Arkansas Democrat*, March 6, 1947.

CHAPTER ELEVEN

1. "Clinton Wins Presidency," *Hot Springs Sentinel Record*, November 4, 1992.

2. Maxine Jones, *Call Me Madam* (Little Rock: Pioneer Press, 1983), 82.

CHAPTER TWELVE

1. "Gambling's Benefits to Hot Springs Reported to be Considerable," *Arkansas Gazette*, December 12, 1960.

2. "Chicago Sheriff Critical of Hot Springs," *Arkansas Gazette*, October 31, 1963.

3. Bob Lancaster, "Cosmopolitan Oasis," *Arkansas Gazette*, December 10, 1991.

4. "Why Does Arkansas Allow Gambling in Hot Springs?" *Crossett News Observer* (AR), March 8, 1964.

5. "Biggest Non-Floating Dice Game," *New York Daily News*, March 15, 1964.

6. "Judge Orders Doors of Casinos Closed, Police Will Comply," *Arkansas Gazette*, March 28, 1964.

7. "Casino Head Says Gambling is Good for the State," *Arkansas Gazette*, November 5, 1964.

8. All Britton, *Leo and Verne*, 595.

9. "No Dice in Hot Springs," *Saturday Evening Post*, September 19, 1964.

10. Allbritton, *Leo and Verne*, 597.

11. Allbritton, *Leo and Verne*, 595.

12. "Big Spenders Bypass Law-Abiding Resort," *Arkansas Democrat*, December 14 1964.

13. "Spa Judge Aware of Gambling," *Arkansas Democrat*, April 2, 1965.

14. "Open Gambling Rolls On," *Arkansas Democrat*, May 5, 1965.

CHAPTER THIRTEEN

1. Editorial, *Arkansas Democrat*, February 5, 1974.
2. Doug Smith, quoted in "Who Says Nobody Comes to Hot Springs Anymore," *Arkansas Gazette*, November 8, 1980.
3. "Hot Springs Beats Paris Jet Set," W, January 1987, 16.

CHAPTER FOURTEEN

1. "Hot Springs Promotes Its Arts Scene," *Arkansas Democrat-Gazette*, October 1, 1993.
2. "Lincoln Statue Draws Protest," *Arkansas Democrat-Gazette*, September 5, 2003.
3. "Deciding What's Hot in the Spa City," *Arkansas Democrat-Gazette*, September 26, 2004.

INDEX

Aldrich, A. R., 64
Alligator Farm, 51, 158
Arkansas Democrat, 126, 130, 144, 145
Arkansas Democrat-Gazette, 157, 158
Arkansas Gazette, 6, 7, 9, 10, 132, 135, 137
Arkansas Trust, 149
Atkins, Homer, 113, 115
Arlington Hotel, 26, 29, 32, 37, 54, 85, 86, 87, 96, 102, 110, 119
Army and Navy Hospital, xi, 1, 33, 39, 73, 79, 85, 100, 116, 118, 119, 120, 122, 123, 126, 128, 135, 142, 151
Arrison, Steve, 157
Austin Hotel, 64

Bailey, Carl, 108
Bailey, W. T., 64
Bathhouse Row, 20, 46, 75, 117
Barkeloo, William, 9
Belding, Ludovicus, 6, 13, 16
Belverdere Club, 140
Black Orchid, 151
Bojangles, 121
Boston Red Sox, 49, 159
Breland, Keller, 134
Brooklyn Dodgers, 49
Buckstaff Bathhouse, 66, 157

Caddo Indians, ix
Campbell, H. T. 51
Capone, Al, 96, 105
Carey, James, 93
Caraway, Hattie, 111
Cates, Issac, 5
Central Avenue, 29, 48, 86, 119, 155
Cherry, Francis, 131
Chicago Cubs, 49
Chicago & Southwestern Air Line, 124
Chicago 400 Journal of Topics, 37, 48
Chistianson, Bertha, 64

Chitwood, George, 61, 62, 63, 67
Chitwood, Oscar, 61, 62, 63, 67
Civil War, 12, 13
Cleaf, Van, 17, 20, 21, 22
Clinton, Bill, 137, 158
Colliers, 101, 102, 107
COMO Hotel, 78, 119, 152
Connelly, Maurice, 84
Crane, Stephen, x
Crystal Bathhouse, 64
Cutter, Charles, 24, 25

Daughters of the Confederacy, 118
Dempsey, Jack, 98
de Soto, Hernando, xi, 1, 114
DeSoto Hotel, 118
DeSoto Valley Springs, 29
Dobbs, P. E., 144
Doran, S. A., 30, 31, 32, 33, 36
Dugan Stuart Building, 159
Dunbar, William, 2, 3, 5

Eastman, George, 34
Eastman Hotel, 34, 39, 119, 122
Eisele, Martin, 65
Essex Park, 56

Faubus, Orval, 131, 136, 137, 140, 143, 144
Featherstonhaugh, George, 7, 8
Floyd, Jim, 92
Flynn, Jack, 32
Flynn, Frank, 29, 31, 32, 36
Fordyce Bathhouse, 75, 103, 110
Fordyce, Samuel, 29, 30, 31, 37, 47, 75, 87
Fox, Frank, 70
Fry, C. W., 37
Futrell, Marion, 111

Gaines block, 149
Gaines, L. S., 33

Gannaway, James, 144
Gardner, Robert, 70
Garrett, A. S., 33
Garvan Gardens, 155
Garvan, Vera, 156
Goodine, John, 70
Gordon, Will, 36
Goslee, Tom, 37, 41
Government Free Bathhouse, 63
Great Northern Hotel, 127

Hale Bathhouse, 34, 147
Hale, John, 13
Hammond, Will, 9
Happy Hollow, 92, 108
Harpers, 17, 20
Harris, Dane, 140, 141, 143
Hart, Jim, 43, 45
Head, Frank, 73
Hinkle, Louis, 41
Hoover, J. W., 108
Hot Springs Bathhouse Association, 28
Hot Springs Bathhouse, 54
Hot Springs Creek, 28
Hot Springs Daily Hornet, 27
Hot Springs Daily News, 35
Hot Springs Documentary Film
    Festival, 154
Hot Springs Illustrated Monthly News,
    22, 23
Hot Springs Mountain, 18
Hot Springs Mountain Tower, 57, 116,
    151
Hot Springs National Park, 81, 159
Hot Springs Railway Company, 26
Hot Springs Sentinel Record, 22, 38,
    58, 59, 73, 74, 83, 103, 135
Houpt, Jake, 61, 62, 63
Houpt, Sid, 61
Housely, Floyd, 139
Houston, Sam, 7
Howard Hotel, 80
Hunley, William, 142
Hunter, George, 2, 3

Imperial Bathhouse, 39
Imperial Hotel, 38
Indiana Club, 71

Iron Mountain Railroad, 52, 53
IQ Zoo, 134

Jaccards Jewelry, 82, 97
Jacobs, W. S., 96, 101, 102, 105, 107
Jefferson, Thomas, 1, 2, 3, 5
Jodd, M. H., 64
Jones, Maxine, 131
Josephine Toussaud Wax Museum, 148

Karpis, Alvin "Creepy," 108
Klondike Saloon, 37, 42
Knickerbocker Hotel, 159, 160
Knights of Pythias, 64
Kress, 79
Kulp, Benjamin, 157

Lamar Bathhouse, 147
Lane, Jim, 29, 30, 31
Lancaster, Bob, 137
LaSalle, 1
Ledgerwood, Vernal, 53
Lefler, Edmund, 27
Linde, T. F., 27
Little Rock and Hot Springs Railroad,
    47
Livingston, Robert, 1
Louisiana Purchase, ix, 2
Luciano, "Lucky," 108
Lyceum Theater, 74

Magic Springs Park, 157
Majestic Hotel, 50, 118
Malvern, AR, 2, 19, 35, 115
Markel, Paul, 90, 91
Market Street Garage, 77
Matthews, Charles, 27, 28, 29
Maurice Bathhouse, 65, 68, 147
Maurice, William, 65, 66, 67
McClard's BBQ, 98
McClellan, John, 136, 138
McLaughlin, Leo, 81, 101, 105, 106,
    108, 109, 113, 120, 124, 126, 133
McMath, Sid, 123, 125, 126, 128
McPherson, Aimee Semple, 106
Medial Arts Building, 159
Mellard, Joseph, 6
Military Redistribution Center, 118

Mitchell, Arthur, 113
Moody Hotel, 60, 140, 150
Mountain Valley Hotel, 104

Napoleon, 1
National Baptist Hotel, 156
National Baseball School, 89
National Park Service, 137
News Observer, 135
New York Daily News, 138
Nuttall, Thomas, 5

Oaklawn Park, 56, 69, 159
Ohio Club, 145
Ostrich Farm, 80
Ouachita River, 2, 5, 73
Ozark Bathhouse, 147

Palace Bathhouse, 30
Park Hotel, 52, 118
Perciful, John, 5
Peterson, Charles, 101
Pike, Albert, 25
Pinkerton, William, 85
Princess Theater, 73
Prohibition, 69, 77, 92
Pythian Bathhouse, 121
Public Opinion, 105

Quapaw Bathhouse, 147, 157, 159

Rector, Henry, 10, 16
Rector House hotel, 10, 27
Reynolds, "Diamond" Joe, 9, 35, 47, 139
Roane, Julie, 13
Roanoke Baptist Church, 76
Robinson, Joe T., 85, 99, 109
Rockefeller, Winthrop, 142, 143, 145, 146
Rockafellow Bathhouse, 41
Rooney, Mickey, 145
Roosevelt, Eleanor, 111

Roosevelt, Franklin, 109, 110, 111
Roosevelt, Teddy, 72
Rugg, D. C., 29
Ruth, Babe, 36, 49

Saint Charles Hotel, 150
Saint Joseph's Infirmary, 56, 94, 117
Saturday Evening Post, 123, 141, 143
Sevier, Ambrose, 6
Schneck's, 79
Schumann, Clarence, 67
Smith, Doug, 148
Smith, Kate, 104
Social Hygiene Board, 81
Southern Grill, 96, 97, 141, 142, 143, 146, 160
Steele, Gen. Frederick, 11
Sumpter Hotel, 14
Superior Bathhouse, 147

Teeter, P. T., 47
Toller, Tom, 32, 36, 41, 42, 43, 45
True Democrat, 10

US Public Health Service, 81

Valentino, Rudolph, 98
Vapors Club, 135, 140, 141, 144
venereal disease, 6, 81
Vint, Thomas, 101

Ward, Jimmy, 69, 70
Wenger, Oliver, 81
Wheatley, Hill, 149
White Front Club, 145
Whittington, Emma, 45
Whittington, Hiram, 7, 8, 13
Whittington Park, 43, 44
Williams, Coffee, 36
Williams, Robert, 36, 41, 43, 45
Wisconsin-Arkansas Lumber Co., 156
Wolf, Dan, 142